MW00852260

WRITE HARD, DIE FREE

Dispatches from the Battlefields & Barrooms
of the Great Alaska Newspaper War

Howard Weaver

EPICENTER PRESS

Epicenter is a regional press publishing nonfiction books about the arts, history, environment, and diverse cultures and lifestyles of Alaska and the Pacific Northwest.

Publisher: Kent Sturgis
Acquisitions Editor: Lael Morgan
Manuscript Editor: Kent Sturgis
Proofreader: Sherrill Carlson
Cover design: Victoria Michael
Text design: Stephanie Martindale, Anita Jones
Printer: McNaughton & Gunn

Title page photo: Managing Editor Tom Gibboney (left), the author, and staff writer Allan Dodds Frank at The Club China Doll on Fifth Avenue in Anchorage, which served as a home away from home for much of the small staff of the *Anchorage Daily News* in the 1970s.

Photo credits: front cover, Paul Estabrook; back cover, top photo, Ken Roberts; bottom photo, *Anchorage Daily News*. All text photos are from the author's collection, except as otherwise credited: page 86, top, U.S. Army Corps of Engineers, bottom, Abbott Collection; page 87, top left, Abbott Collection, right, Elaine Warren; page 88, bottom, Abbott Collection; page 89, top, *Anchorage Daily News*; page 90, Abbott Collection; page 180, Abbott Collection; page 181, bottom, *Anchorage Daily News*; page 183, Paul Helmar Collection; page 186, bottom, Bill Kossen.

Text ©2012 by Howard Weaver, dba Rosebud Creative LLC, all rights reserved. No part of this publication may be reproduced, stored in a retrieval system, or transmitted in any form or by any means, electronic, mechanical, photocopying, recording, or otherwise, without the prior written permission of the publisher. Permission is given for brief excerpts to be published with book reviews in newspapers, magazines, newsletters, catalogs, and online publications.

Library of Congress Control Number: 2012934020
ISBN 978-1-935347-19-4

10 9 8 7 6 5 4 3 2 1
Printed in the United States of America

To order single copies of WRITE HARD, DIE FREE, mail $14.95 plus $6 for shipping (WA residents add $1.90 state sales tax) to Epicenter Press, PO Box 82368, Kenmore, WA 98028; call us at 800-950-6663, or visit www.EpicenterPress.com. Find *Epicenter Press Alaska Book Adventures* on Facebook.

More photos, documents, and a searchable database of the text of this book may be found at www.writeharddiefree.com.

To Jeff,
Love Dad

Like my career, this memoir owes its existence to the generosity and assistance of many people, but this dedication belongs to one person alone: Barbara Hodgin, my wife and companion, with whom I have shared so many adventures. I cannot do justice to her contributions, nor adequately express my gratitude to her.

Without you, Barb, none of this would have mattered.

Contents

Preface 7

Introduction 9

1. Love at first sight 13
2. Adrift in the demimonde 19
3. Anointed Boy Reporter 23
4. Fat, dumb, and happy 29
5. Becoming investigative 37
6. Pulitzer lightning 49
7. Our own newspaper 55
8. Encore for a Pulitzer 61
9. The virtues of excess 65
10. Music in the cafes at night 75
11. Learning fast at the end 83
12. A bugle, then the cavalry 95
13. Bright and cheerful colors 103
14. It wasn't an accident 107
15. The distant emperor 113
16. America's best newsroom 121
17. The talent show 127
18. Alaska's tribal fire 135
19. Looking around the corners 153
20. Thirsty 165
21. A People in Peril 171
22. A journalistic oil slick 187
23. In harm's way 199
24. Bleeding Bill Allen 205
25. My new narrative 215

Photos 86

More Photos 180

Epilogue 223

Author's note 227

Acknowledgments 231

Index 233

About the author 239

Preface

I think of this work neither as my autobiography nor a scholarly history of the *Anchorage Daily News* and *Alaska Advocate*. Instead it is a recollection of the time I spent at those fine newspapers and an opportunity to share my memories of how our improbable victory in the Alaska Newspaper War came to pass.

Many people and events crucial to that success are absent in this chronicle, which I have constrained and streamlined in hopes of offering a coherent narrative. The star of the story is meant to be the quest for decent journalism against imposing odds.

I've quoted extensively from the contemporaneous notes and memos I saved in an effort to report previously undisclosed details about how we fought these battles. Although this account is as factually accurate as I can make it, many of the conclusions are, of course, my opinion. Unlike most historians, I was an active and anything but impartial combatant.

The successes we enjoyed never could have come to pass without the talent, dedication, and participation of innumerable colleagues, friends, and supporters whose names would fill many pages. I'm sorry they are not all memorialized here.

If you don't like what I've written here, I'm sorry about that, too. But I promised myself I'd tell the truth as clearly as I know it.

Any mistakes or misperceptions are, of course, entirely my own.

Introduction

The strategies and tactics that would come to define American newspaper wars first surfaced at the dawn of the Twentieth Century in New York City, where press lords named Hearst and Pulitzer fought a blistering competition that introduced the country to the penny press, Yellow Journalism, and muckraking. As newspaper circulations surged, the owners became as rich and powerful as they were arrogant.

This fierce competition also fostered enormous public service, giving voice to immigrants and the working class while fighting for public health, safety, and sanitation. As the country's foremost press critic A.J. Liebling would observe later, "Competitive newspapers love the little guy; his name is Circulation."

Like today's battles amongst reality television programs, newspaper competitions often resulted in sensationalism and excess. A month after purchasing his first newspaper in San Francisco, William Randolph Hearst's *Examiner* headlined the story of a hotel fire like this:

HUNGRY, FRANTIC FLAMES

They Leap Madly Upon the Splendid
Pleasure Palace by the Bay of Monterey,

Encircling Del Monte in Their Ravenous
Embrace from Pinnacle to Foundation

Pulitzer's *New York World* in New York City reported on the perils of the poor during a record heat wave with stories like "How Babies Are Baked," and "A Row of Little Hearses."

When Hearst bought the *New York Journal* in 1895 to challenge the mighty *World* he adopted business tactics that became standard practice, including lowering the price of the newspaper (in his case, to a penny) and hiring away the best staffers from the opposition. It was just such a competition for a popular cartoon strip, "The Yellow Kid," that gave rise to the label "yellow journalism."

Still later in cities such as Chicago, Detroit, Seattle, Miami, San Francisco, and Buffalo, newspaper wars grew even hotter, sometimes involving gunfire and sabotage as competing circulation drivers squared off and alliances were formed with organized crime to ensure delivery. Reporters became the brawling, hard-drinking foot soldiers in these wars, as adept at stealing photographs from a victim's parlor wall as disabling a competitor's telephone.

The arrival of television as a mass medium after World War II marked the beginning of the end of fiercely competitive daily newspapers in America. Evening television news generally spelled the end of afternoon newspapers, which either folded or consolidated with successful morning rivals. The remaining papers enjoyed the traditional benefit of monopolists — including obscene profits — but too often lost their edge for unbridled competition or the championing of ordinary readers.

The newspaper wars did not end overnight, and the era did not pass silently away. In cities across the country, stubborn owners and devoted staffers soldiered on while they could but eventually fell one after another to the imperatives of modern media economics. Soon the storied battles were mostly history and only a few continued.

Lucky for me, one of the last and most vigorous of these battles was fought on the streets of my hometown of Anchorage,

Alaska, where I spent the first twenty years of my newspaper career in a rough and rollicking rumble that Hearst and Pulitzer would have recognized in an instant. By the time it ended it 1992 we had employed most of the tactics that had emerged in earlier classic confrontations and learned lessons new generations of journalists will be forced to learn in other arenas.

Chapter One
Love at first sight

Long before the end of my first year in a real newsroom, I knew my teenage marriage wasn't going to survive it. By the end of the next year, my young bride knew it too.

The first time she choked back tears and sobbed, "You love that damned newsroom more than you love me," I must have waited a split-second too long before denying it. She never brought it up again and I never admitted it, but by the time I moved out we both knew it was true.

My affection for the newsroom at the *Anchorage Daily News* was instantaneous and my devotion never faltered. Like Paul on the road to Damascus, I was struck down by revelation: I belonged here, soaking up the well-blended cocktail of cynicism and idealism in a smoky room that looked a little like those news photos of trailer parks after a tornado. The mundane world of city streets and Rotary Club meetings was eclipsed by a daily miracle of storytelling fueled by equal parts of urgency, insecurity, and ambition. No matter what you were before, here you could become a byline, privileged to add your words to those being delivered every day to doorsteps all over town.

"Come on, kid," a veteran said after deadline one night. "We're done here; let's go get drunk and be somebody."

I was all for drinking, but I already felt like somebody: Staff Writer. It said so right under my name, often several times in a single edition. My dad, when he was sober enough to notice, was proud of me, and sometimes I didn't feel like the poor kid from a shabby neighborhood any more. I couldn't imagine ever giving up this feeling.

Yet inside I remained an insecure kid from Muldoon, and one day I would understand that the newsroom I adored was filled with fuck-ups and fragile egos every bit as twisted as my own. Nobody came to work in an under-staffed, under-paid, over-worked newsroom at the dying number two daily in Anchorage, Alaska because they'd selected it over all their other bright prospects.

A few, like me, were young and hungry, learning something every day and still naive enough to believe this was a launching pad, not a warehouse. Others were not.

Everybody was a drinker, most were divorced or headed in that direction, and as far as I knew only one person—the editor—owned a home. The apartments and old rental houses we shared were interchangeably shabby: cramped and aged quarters filled with musty rust-colored carpets and slightly molding furniture—where there was any furniture at all. Wobbly old refrigerators were full of cheap beer, the cabinets held whiskey, and our medicine chests contained extra-large bottles of Extra Strength Excedrin, often with the top removed and simply thrown away. A gray film of accumulated cigarette smoke coated the inside of every window; unless the living room smelled like Patchouli oil, it smelled of tobacco and cheap marijuana.

There was no desk available when I started at the *Daily News*. Instead, I shifted around the small, crowded newsroom to occupy whatever spot was vacant at the moment; I got up and moved without being asked when the venerable veterans returned. I couldn't touch-type (still can't) and sometimes I got stuck with an old manual typewriter where the most frequently used keys had been worn smooth. Was this the "a" or the "s" key under my finger? Which is the "r" and which the "t"?

A few months after my arrival, an old-timer—he was probably thirty-five, I realize now— passed me in the hallway on his way out. "Looks like you got a desk now, kid," he told me.

That was Dan, a frequent lunchtime Martini drinker and would-be novelist who had just finished a spectacular series on big-game bandits, the ruthless mercenary guides who broke all the rules in leading trophy hunters—usually tourists—to prized kills. His florid, sanguinary descriptions and withering analysis had caused upheaval at the state Department of Fish and Game and brought telephoned death threats to the newsroom. I was stunned to be told he'd just been fired. I never learned why, but I moved my stuff into his desk later that afternoon.

The city editor delighted in my clumsiness and rookie anxiety and loved to hiss "pressure, pressure ... deadline, deadline" while flicking paperclips that bounced off the back of my head. Despite my lack of typing skill or experience, I turned out to be a fast, clean writer and within a few months could frustrate his sport by turning in copy that not only satisfied the editors but often made it onto the front page.

Except for the sports section, I was the only local with a byline. I could tell that some older colleagues thought of me as a kind of teacher's pet, perhaps the newsroom mascot, but they didn't mind that my uninterrupted, voluminous production took some pressure off of them to fill the paper's newshole. It wasn't uncommon for veterans to "reassign" to me stories they didn't want to cover. I always said yes, always came back with something and occasionally surprised them and the editors by coming back with something good.

The characters I worked with in that newsroom could have been cast for the film *The Front Page* — and many cultivated their eccentricities. Many images spring readily to mind: Molly Bowditch, who'd worked at Time magazine, was an unlikely, sophisticated transplant from Mount Holyoke College. ("They taught us to pronounce it like 'the whole yolk of an egg'," she once explained.) She smoked Pall Malls and filled her tiny rented house with Great

Danes. Allan Frank, instantly recognizable by a mop of tangled hair and perpetually frantic demeanor, was a big-city boy, a graduate of Columbia Journalism School whose father in New York City ran *Family Weekly*, one of the newspaper industry's biggest Sunday supplements. Jeanne Montague—soon to become Jeanne Abbott, the editor's wife—was only a bit older than me but behaved with poise I admired across the tattered newsroom. Elaine Warren was a winsome girl about my age who seemed infinitely more worldly than I. Though her grandfather had mined for gold in Juneau, and her dad was born there, she had lived in California and was a stylish writer and dresser who drove a Karmann Ghia. At the next desk was A. Cameron Edmonson, who invariably asked "marrying or burying?" whenever I showed up with a necktie and who wore a watch on his ankle to keep track of time as he sat cross-legged and churned out business stories.

Our bosses weren't that much older than their staffers and certainly were no less strange. Tom Brown—he'd been a foreign correspondent!—brought six feet, six inches of talent, energy, and cynicism to the city desk. He moved our typewritten copy to the production department by slamming open a sliding plexiglass window and shouting "Eat it up, you rats" as he tossed it into a wire basket. Tom Gibboney was managing editor but like everybody handled multiple duties; he edited the sports page or the front page with equal panache and once admitted to me that he had washed out of officer candidate school in the Army because he "lacked respect for authority."

The big boss was Stan Abbott, our executive editor and a steadfast mentor who opened more doors for me than I realized until much later. He'd hired me as a stringer when he was sports editor and I was a sixteen-year-old high school junior, ordering up stories on wrestling matches and hockey games that paid about five dollars each and—far more important—put my byline in the paper. Seemingly equal parts Jack Kerouac and Jack Daniels, he loomed large in my career until his departure years later, which likewise opened an important door for me.

Outside the newsroom the most important people in my world were at the Club China Doll: proprietor Louis "Jiggs" Giggliotti and cocktail waitress Loma Bording, who tirelessly fetched drinks and flirted until our paychecks were gone or Jiggs' patience was exhausted.

In my early days the paper still largely reflected the legacy of legendary Chicago newsman Larry Fanning, the editor and publisher who'd died a classic newsman's deadline death at his desk in the same newsroom a year before I arrived. We believed in gangsters and crooked politicians and breathless headlines. Struggling one night for the right headline for photos of a remote shipwreck and rescue—DRAMA IN THE FOG, one proposed; another liked LIFE AND DEATH IN THE NORTH PACIFIC—editors finally asked Larry for help. He immediately turned and dictated: FIRST PICTURES OF ALEUTIAN RESCUE.

In his legacy newsroom I learned to write every story to its limit—and sometimes a step or two beyond. A barroom killing at the Beef & Bourbon nightclub early in my career became "the double shotgun slaying" in every reference thereafter, and I still have the folder of notes and tips with which I fully expected to solve the case myself. (I didn't).

When Gary Zieger, the younger brother of a high school friend, was charged in a gruesome murder, I was ready.

The victim—a fetching young woman with the made-for-headlines name of ZeZe Mason—was discovered stabbed to death in an isolated gravel pit on the edge of town, and Zieger was charged on the basis of classic who-done-it circumstantial evidence. He was guilty by virtue of his reputation amongst the city cops and was suspected of other more hideous killings. The two talented young Public Defenders who handled his case won a change of venue to Kodiak, an island town in the Gulf of Alaska, on account of our coverage, resulting in my first out-of-town assignment. The city's dominant daily, the *Anchorage Times*, wouldn't spring for airfare to send a reporter, so I would have the story to myself. (The veteran court reporter I competed against was jealous but not spiteful, collegially advising me to take along a receipt book and two different colored pens to give my expense reports more credibility.)

Communications in Alaska were still primitive in the early 1970s, and I suspect I might have been one of the last newspaper reporters in the country to file stories by telegraph, as I did from Kodiak. In those days before Alaskans had access even to the primitive Telecopier fax machine that Hunter S. Thompson dubbed the Mojo Wire, I had to finish each day's story between the end of the court session, at 3:30 or 4 p.m., and the closing of the telegraph office at 6 p.m.

That left no time to travel out the road to the house where I was staying (at no cost to the newspaper) with a friend of a friend, so I set up shop at a little round table in a corner of Tony's Bar, cranking out coverage on the portable typewriter my uncle had carried throughout the Korean War. The trial lasted almost three weeks, and my daily visit soon became a feature at Tony's, where a pretty dancer named Jeanne and other employees began to cluster around the table for a daily update when I arrived.

As much as this played into my Damon Runyon fantasies, I worried at first about wasting time with my unbreakable telegraph deadline looming. After a few days, though, I learned to use their reactions to help organize and shape my stories before I started writing, highlighting the scenes that captured their attention—an early example, perhaps, of crowd-sourcing.

I'd always been more interested in writing for the readers than for the copy desk, and the success of my front-page exclusives from Tony's Bar day after day did little to tone me down. Gary Zieger was found not guilty after his lawyers produced a surprise witness who said she'd seen ZeZe alive after the time prosecutors fixed for the killing—a storybook ending I wish I had written as well as its Raymond Chandler plot deserved.

I got better, though, and a year or so later Gary Zieger was to figure prominently in the best crime story and one of the best leads I ever wrote.

Chapter Two

Adrift in the demimonde

I settled comfortably into the crime beat, mining the naturally colorful Alaska characters and still-rugged frontier atmosphere of my hometown for a steady stream of genuine if slightly hyperventilated stories. Soon enough I moved on to writing series that allowed me to wander even wider: "Heroin in Anchorage" and "The Mob Moves In" were typical examples from the early 1970s.

The prevalence of heroin addiction in Anchorage wouldn't have registered as big news in most urban settings, but I knew with native certainty how it would play locally. Simply by pointing out that the same drugs found in big U.S. cities could be found in our hometown was shocking to most readers. It didn't hurt that our competition, though much bigger, was a newspaper of little ambition and even less interest in the problems of ordinary people. I didn't have to write "The Man with the Golden Arm" to shock our readers, though God knows I tried.

On the other hand, Anchorage residents were not surprised to hear that sex was on sale in our town, the subject of our next series about massage parlors. In a boom-and-bust town with large military bases and perhaps five men for every woman, prostitution was hardly news. We managed to create a stir anyhow.

Alaska's traditional whorehouses—gold-rush fixtures that lasted well into the Twentieth Century—usually were sedate and all-but-public businesses, often operating in residential houses clustered together on the outskirts of town, along what longtime Anchorage residents called "The Line." In the early '70s, however, massage parlors in Anchorage were proliferating, highly visible establishments that advertised openly and seemed to flaunt their operations. One advertised with the motto "It's a business doing pleasure with you."

Allan Frank and I were convinced there was more to this story than sex for sale. I had covered a celebrated murder trial in which the successful defense claimed the killing actually was fallout from an effort by organized crime to control and extort the parlors, and we had found evidence to demonstrate that convincingly, if not infallibly. What made our series work for readers was our approach, which included sending women from the newsroom in for job interviews and publishing detailed accounts of what they found there. Elaine Warren's account of her interview began, "Wearing my raciest outfit and an ounce of perfume ..." I can't recall her perfume but I retain a distinct memory of that racy outfit.

I learned a new word from Allan along the way: verisimilitude. In order to write the stories authentically, he argued, we had to spend some time as customers in the parlors ourselves, so he made a number of solo visits that he described as research. I was with him later when we went into Linda's Massage late one night looking for an on-the-record interview.

Yes, it was 3 a.m., but that was mid-day in the massage parlor business. We announced ourselves as reporters upon arrival and asked to speak to the proprietor. The large man who came out to refuse our request was not amused, but Allan's persistence finally brought "Linda" herself out to the lobby.

"Persistence" is of course a euphemism; Allan was in full-throated New Yorker mode by then: insistent, insulting, and loud. He screamed at the man to butt out. We wanted to speak directly to Linda, a short middle-aged Korean woman who feigned a lack of English and had nothing to say to us. "What is he, your pimp?" Allan demanded.

As far as I can tell, that was what triggered the phone call to police; not long afterward two of Anchorage's finest crowded into the small waiting room and tried to calm the situation.

No, they wouldn't arrest us; they couldn't see that there was any crime here. But, yes, they were sure we'd be happy to leave quietly—a recommendation I wholeheartedly endorsed. "If you want them arrested, you'll have to place them under citizen's arrest," an officer told Linda. "If there's any crime here it's trespassing, and we don't arrest on misdemeanors unless they take place in our presence."

That seemed like a fine exit line to me; instead, Allan got into Linda's face and kept yelling, "If you want me arrested, arrest me. Don't waste my time!" Her English improved instantly as she announced "I place you under citizen's arrest." Moments later we were in handcuffs on our way out the door.

We were surprised to see the local ABC station's high-profile news director standing in the street, lights blazing and camera rolling. "When I heard 'Frank' and 'Weaver' on the police scanner I didn't believe it," he told me later. "But you know, it never hurts to check."

We spent the next eight hours in a drunk tank that smelled like puke and Lysol, an experience that was nonetheless more pleasant than my subsequent meetings with Publisher Kay Fanning or, later still, my wife. I proclaimed my innocence in both sessions. "If we'd been spending any money," I explained, "they would have never called the police."

Later that May afternoon in 1973 the *Anchorage Times* took notice, as well. I thought the one-column, two paragraph story was remarkably restrained—a lot different than what I'd have written. I still have the clipping.

POLICE ARREST TWO REPORTERS

Two reporters for the Anchorage Daily News, Allan Frank
and Howard Weaver, were arrested and charged with

trespassing early this morning at Linda's Massage Parlor, 2808 Eureka Street.

Chapter Three
Anointed Boy Reporter

In the early 1970s Alaska was poised between its gold-rush past and the coming tumult of trans-Alaska pipeline construction, a coltish adolescent society where the booze, gambling and prostitution of its past were beginning to seem a quaint legacy in light of tougher, bloodier operations then emerging. It was a splendid time to be a crime reporter.

I wanted to refer to Anchorage's traditional criminal establishment as "disorganized crime" to distinguish it from the tougher new guys, but the editors wouldn't allow it. Still, the old guard remained my primary focus in early years, a deeply rooted and uniquely local brand of roués, pimps, and con men who operated essentially in the open, a fact of life most Anchorage citizens would readily acknowledge. Many people still played "the numbers" in those pre-lotto days, wagering small sums daily with the aid of runners who took their bets to the "policy bank" and delivered the infrequent winnings. The main bank was operated—by right of inheritance—by the son of a local underworld figure, just like other new generations of up-and-coming business leaders—Eddie Rasmussen at the National Bank of Alaska or Elaine Atwood at the *Anchorage Times,* for example. He was another local kid working his way up in the family business.

I quickly learned that he and other local gangsters secretly enjoyed occasional press coverage as it conferred status among their peers. (Later I would learn this wasn't a new insight. "The reputation of power is power," Voltaire had observed.) Local detectives already knew more about all of them than I would ever report, so I was a problem for them only if my coverage forced unwanted enforcement on account of public pressure. (Bringing down the heat unnecessarily didn't do me any good either.) Soon enough I was a familiar face in their barroom haunts and after-hours gambling parlors, where they'd usually talk, frequently lie, and sometimes tell me secrets.

This was irresistible to me, an ever-so-slightly dangerous world populated with colorful characters, naked dancers, and plenty to drink. I learned to spot the cheaters at the felt-covered Panguini table in the Union Club – or thought I could. I knew Put Your Hat On Brown, a reliable, small-time drug dealer who always wore his fedora out into the alley to conduct business. Customers approached him at the bar to initiate a buy with the admonition, "Put your hat on, Brown." I rode through nighttime streets in a patrol car with one of my best friends, a city cop, and sat up late telling stories in Station One with another, a young fireman.

I had the field pretty much to myself. The *Anchorage Times* was by every measure an establishment newspaper; writing about the city's abundant drug dealers or flamboyant hookers wouldn't have gone over well at the First Presbyterian Church or the Downtown Rotary. These elements had no place in the chamber of commerce's public image of Anchorage, a pristine and constipated place that would be, as they might announce, "BIG Anchorage—Business Is Good."

The city fathers had no aversion to visiting hookers or card-rooms, mind you, but they shared an inviolate taboo against talking about it. As *Times* Publisher Robert B. Atwood would tell interviewers in 1975, "We don't report the arrests of professional people—we give them the soft treatment..."

That was a policy that left a lot of room for a reporter like me.

Looking back, I find even more anonymous sources in my stories than I remembered. Rules about using them were loose or non-existent in those days—after all, the Watergate exposé just then was unfolding in Washington—and a local boy like me could find talkative insiders everywhere. Often my "source close to the investigation" might be nothing more than a patrolman I'd gone to high school with telling me something he overheard some detective saying, but I was honest about how I used them and the tips were almost always right.

About this time I read Peter Matthiessen's book, *At Play in the Fields of the Lord,* whose title perfectly described my nights in the Anchorage demimonde. I produced a steady flow of stories that played on the front page and brought home Alaska Press Club awards. Once in a while I was able to reach a little deeper, exposing how an assistant district attorney was manipulating a grand jury investigation, catching a corrupt city manager, or showing a clear pattern of favoritism in the award of state transportation contracts. I was twenty-three and every day was Christmas.

Maybe some of it went to my head. A competitor at the *Times* once mailed a letter addressed to "Anointed Boy Reporter/ *Anchorage Daily News*" and, sure enough, it showed up on my desk.

Okay, I was self-righteous, but I was genuinely righteous, too. These stories were the early expressions of a lifelong passion for fairness and egalitarianism that would motivate my journalism for forty years. I celebrated ordinary people and never passed an opportunity to stick it to the big shots. Think of it as Muldoon's revenge, a legacy of my threadbare boyhood in a working-class Anchorage neighborhood.

A few years later I was invited to speak at the roast of a prominent political lawyer, the audience a Who's Who of Anchorage society that was by definition foreign turf for me. I was determined to do well, worked hard on my remarks, and hit a home run. Afterward, Alaska's first lady, Ermalee Hickel, introduced herself and said, "I don't think we've met, and I've spent all night trying to place your accent. Where did you come from?"

"Muldoon," I told her.

"I can't believe we've never met," said Mrs. Hickel, herself Anchorage born.

"I don't know," I replied, perhaps unfairly contrasting my working-class roots with hers. "Did you spend much time at the Carpenters Hall?"

I had inherited more than blue-collar roots from my dad, who worked as a carpenter — union and non-union — all over the state. He'd left Texas Tech after a year to join the Navy and fight in the South Pacific, but he nurtured a love of learning for the rest life. I brought home my textbooks after college each year for him to read, and our subsequent discussions often demonstrated that he'd read them more carefully than I.

His view of politics and economics fell somewhere to the left of Franklin Roosevelt, whom he adored, a posture sometimes at odds with my smart, far more ambitious mother. Though alcohol would claim him at an early age (as, indeed, it did my mother) in the early years he planted seeds of egalitarianism and social justice that guided both his sons.

By the time of my conversation with the first lady, I'd left street crime behind to cover politics, but the lessons I'd learned after dark applied for the rest of my career. One of them I shared frequently in later years when asked to speak at graduation ceremonies.

"There's nobody in charge out here. There is no Wizard in the land of Oz. Behind the booming voices and impressive facades, there is usually just a person much like you," I told the graduates.

"You will learn that there is no secret handshake; people in high places are not necessarily smarter than you, or more capable. The mayor may be a moron, the governor a genial nobody being manipulated behind the scenes. Don't be intimidated; you can break the barriers, which exist mainly in your mind."

Another lesson came into play repeatedly as we worked to understand and explain how Alaska operated: the basic behaviors and motivations I learned from the denizens of nighttime streets and Anchorage barrooms could be found elsewhere.

For example, for a while in 1973 many old-guard Anchorage gangsters were in a panic, for good reason: a lot of them were being killed. I tallied seven underworld deaths in our relatively small town that year. "A prosperous, fast-growing economy and the promise of an even bigger boom during pipeline construction years have lured Outside [crime] organizers to Alaska," I wrote somewhat breathlessly.

Hyperbolic I may have been, but the people I knew in nightclubs and gambling houses were genuinely scared. I knew that because I could feel my status changing subtlety as I moved among them. Nobody knew exactly what was going on, but everybody was worried. As a potential source of information who regularly circulated between various factions, I had become more valuable. They needed information and thought that I might have it.

Years later Anchorage faced a panic in the banking industry as lenders who had over-extended in anticipation of pipeline riches teetered on the edge of collapse. Bankers who never would have talked to a reporter a year before suddenly became accessible—exactly as the demimonde had reacted before. "What are you hearing?" one might ask. "I heard there were federal bank examiners in town," another would offer, fishing for confirmation.

My lesson: bankers are no different from pimps in that respect. When people get scared, it's always a good time to start asking questions.

The local underworld panic ended in 1973, more or less, after a nightclub owner's wife and stepson were murdered and their presumed killer quickly done away with as well. The lynchpin was none other than Gary Zieger, who was found dead of shotgun wounds a day after the killings and a subsequent arson that failed to cover up the crime.

Because I knew Zieger's brother and had gotten close to his defense team in Kodiak, I was able quickly to reconstruct a narrative of his last day alive, when he knew he had been targeted and searched frantically and unsuccessfully for sanctuary. It was a compelling story that I introduced like this:

"Gary Zieger lay dead alongside the Seward Highway Tuesday, his life of 20 troubled years ended by the shots he waited for all day."

Chapter Four
Fat, dumb, and happy

Although we later called our twenty-year competition with the *Times* "the Great Alaska Newspaper War," we were hardly more than an irritation to them at first. By nearly every measure—circulation, revenue, reputation — the older, established daily ruled in absolute supremacy. Its masthead proclaimed it to be "Alaska's Largest Newspaper," and there was no arguing with that.

So what made it so easy for us to feel motivated and superior, to sense the winds of destiny at our backs? Easy: the *Times* was an awful newspaper—lazy, partisan, and vindictive. Lucky for us, it was also smug, lifeless, and dull.

Like hundreds of other small-town dailies in the 1950s and '60s, the *Times* was exclusively the tribune of the city's commercial elite, voice of the conventional, defender of the status quo. The paper saw no conflict when its editor served simultaneously as president of the chamber of commerce. In the *Anchorage Times*, what was good for business was by definition good for Anchorage.

Times Publisher Robert Atwood had served as chairman of the Alaska Statehood Committee that lobbied for admission to the union in 1959, an exercise that seemed to confirm him as a lifelong booster. Though frustrated in his personal political ambitions (having run for the U.S. senate after statehood and losing),

Atwood remained a campaigner, most notably championing efforts to move the state capital from Juneau, opposing Native campaigns for land claims and fighting ceaselessly to open the state for oil and gas development. Those efforts, like countless lesser campaigns, engendered blizzards of advocacy coverage in the *Times*; the paper supported its allies and attacked its opponents relentlessly.

The *Times'* predictable support for nearly any economic development was full-throated and unembarrassed. Big issues like the drive for statehood or opening the North Slope to oil production of course drew *Times* attention, but so did vaporous pie-in-the-sky proposals. A 1970 proposal to build a domed, climate-controlled city across Cook Inlet from Anchorage— "Seward's Success," it was to be named—was worthy of front-page coverage of its dreamy vision of "a new city to rise on the horizon."

That wasn't unusual behavior. A former Atwood business partner and longtime associate, Locke Jacobs, later told a reporter approvingly that "When this town needed a chamber of commerce-type paper, he (Atwood) did the tricky little things to make it work. When the town had no courage (to grow) he would run every architect's rendering of every proposed new building. He knew half of them would never be built, but it gave other people the confidence to expand."

When it came to big, real projects, the *Times* pulled out the stops. When the first environmental impact statement for the proposed North Slope oil pipeline included the favorable mention of an alternative route across Canada—which would bypass most of Robert Atwood's Alaska—the paper thundered with not one but two 72-point, all-caps headlines on page one:

U.S. HEARS WRONG STORY ON ROUTE FOR PIPELINE, said the first.

AP STORY HURTS STATE, screamed the second.

When workers were getting ready to start construction some years later, the *Times* published word for word a pipeline company press release heralding "the official start" of the project. The actual event—a convoy of trucks crossing the Yukon River to haul freight northward—was little more than a gimmick, an Alyeska PR chief acknowledged later.

Whatever the journalistic logic of its boosterism, the *Times'* crusades were a consistent asset to its owner, who had made millions of dollars in the oilfields.

Atwood got in early, one of fourteen men who filed federal applications for oil leases on the Kenai Moose Range in the early 1950s even though the area was closed to oil exploration at the time. When the area was opened in 1958 their leases were awarded despite a competing claim from Anchorage lawyer James Tallman that had been filed later, when the fields were actually opened. The case ended up in court. Although the Bureau of Land Management, which managed the leases, supported the position of the Atwood group and won in U.S. District Court, the unsuccessful bidder ultimately won on appeal. The matter went all the way up to the Supreme Court of the United States.

Tallman maintained that the early ruling in favor of the BLM, Atwood, and other insiders was political. "It was a predetermined type of result," he said, noting that he knew his prospects were dim when oil companies weighed in on the side of Atwood and his friends when Supreme Court briefs were filed by Abe Fortas (later a Supreme Court justice himself) and Clark Clifford, a legendary Washington power broker who later served as U.S. attorney general. Indeed, the Atwood contingent won on the final decision.

The *Times* routinely allowed its reporters to travel at oil-company expense, not just out into the pipeline territory, but also to winter conferences in sunny locations. Managing Editor Clint Andrews (whose wife frequently covered oil stories for the *Times*) told me the newsroom didn't have a rule forbidding travel freebies, but added, "...if the newsroom was run under a policy, it would be that a free lunch doesn't buy much."

I never knew the *Times* to oppose any pro-development scheme, nor to support any significant environmental cause, regularly employing supposed news articles as well as editorials to get its way. I can't recall a single crusade in the *Times* on the behalf of the disadvantaged or underprivileged in Alaska; in the case of Alaska Native people fighting for their indigenous rights, the *Times* was an active and often mean-spirited opponent.

During debate over the Alaska Native Claims Settlement Act—landmark legislation that ultimately awarded aboriginal Alaskans forty million acres of land and almost a billion dollars— author Mary Clay Berry wrote that the *Times* "played skillfully on not-so-latent racism, bigotry, and greed to orchestrate (opposition to ANCSA) to a fine pitch."

When a congressional committee came to Alaska in October 1969 for a public hearing on the land claims, the *Times* wrote extensively about proposals being crafted by Native leaders and Arthur Goldberg, the former U.S. Supreme Court justice they had hired to help draft legislation. "This Goldberg line that has been fed into the Alaska Native Federation bill is a threat to all the people of the 49th state," Atwood's paper wrote.

That commentary was decried as "gutter journalism" by a visiting congressman from Oklahoma, whom Berry reported was "furious at the *Times*' insinuations that the proposal was a Jewish scheme foisted on dumb Indians."

"The *Times* articulated the views of a powerful clique in Alaska represented by the chambers of commerce throughout the state," Berry wrote in *The Alaska Pipeline: the Politics of Oil and Native Land Claims*, her 1975 book about the pipeline and Native land claims. "Atwood gave these views respectability by putting them into print. He was, one Native leader remarked bitterly, appealing to 'the dark side of human nature.' His editorials opened the floodgates..."

"When it comes to a clash between racism and economic interests, the *Times* often has difficulty making up its mind," Alaska Native leader Roy Huhndorf wryly noted in a 1976 interview.

Economic discrimination also came naturally to the *Times*. As Atwood told the authors of *Lost Frontier: The Marketing of Alaska*, his newspaper didn't report arrests of professional people.

"If they come to trial, we will report that. But accountants, doctors, professional people—we give them soft treatment because their reputations could really be hurt if they're arrested, even if charges are dropped later."

That kind of smugness was an irresistible target for a working-class boy from Muldoon. Home from Johns Hopkins one summer during my undergrad years, I applied for a job covering baseball for the *Anchorage Times*. (I had already tried the *News*, which wasn't hiring). I arrived for an interview with *Times* majordomo Bill Tobin with a collection of my college newspaper clippings in hand, carefully arranged with what I thought were my best stories on top.

Tobin read nothing beyond the first sentence of my first story before exploding. Describing a Vietnam war protest I had covered, my lead said something about events at "a mostly peaceful demonstration" in Baltimore.

"Mostly peaceful?" he asked loudly. "Mostly peaceful?" Louder still.

"I guess I just don't understand the language anymore," he thundered. "How can you call these hoodlums peaceful?"

I was perhaps nineteen or twenty at the time, and being yelled at by the editor of Alaska's largest newspaper was intimidating. Even so, I had the presence of mind to reach across his desk and retrieve my file of clippings before leaving. He was still red-faced, ranting about bums, thugs, and hippies as I walked away.

Certainty of their own virtue and righteousness also insulated *Times* management from the realities of change and would one day set the stage for spectacular defeat, though that was years away at the time of our struggles in the early '70s. The *Times* was winning pretty much every round in those days.

The *Daily News* did enjoy one advantage that was just starting to matter; it was the morning paper. In most of the country, afternoon papers were eroding, damaged by increasing viewership of evening television news and changing cultural habits that sent people to work later in the morning. In Anchorage, neither trend was yet a significant factor.

A large military presence built around thousands of troops and hundreds of good civilian jobs at neighboring Air Force and Army installations influenced the early start of the business day in Anchorage. People who were due at work by 7:30 or 8 a.m. were less likely to read a morning paper. When they got home in the early afternoon, the *Anchorage Times* was waiting for them, while network television news didn't air until 11 p.m., having been recorded in Seattle and flown north for rebroadcast.

Non-news network TV programming in those days was delayed a full two weeks to avoid the expanse of shipping it via air freight. Christmas specials recorded in Seattle were shown in Anchorage in mid-January. The Apollo moon landing—July 20, 1969—was the first live national TV broadcast ever seen in Alaska, and it took news almost that big to break through to live coverage for years to come.

Robert Atwood loudly and frequently proclaimed that a morning paper couldn't work in Alaska, where cold dark mornings made delivery, mainly by kids, far more difficult. Waves of new residents attracted by Alaska's booming economy, most of them arriving from cities where morning papers ruled, would disagree.

The *Times* delivered what should have been the knockout punch in the newspaper competition in August, 1974, when the two papers announced a "joint operating agreement" by which the *Daily News* agreed to permanent commercial subjugation in exchange for editorial survival. Organized under a newly created federal anti-trust exemption designed to save unprofitable papers, the JOA gave the *Times* control over production, advertising, and circulation efforts and required the *News* to turn over its Sunday edition—the only one in the state. In theory, efficiencies and cost savings under the new structure would create profits sufficient for the *News* to maintain an independent newsroom.

Of course I knew nothing about the underlying financial realities, but the deal felt to me like simple failure, a bitter defeat at the hands of the Forces of Darkness. Alongside a sizable collection of colleagues, I started drinking in mid-afternoon the day of announcement and ended the night in an alley behind the *Times* throwing stones at second-story windows. As near as I can recall, none connected; in fact, it would be years before I landed a telling blow.

Over the next five years, the *Times* allowed certain success to slip away, surely the worst (and dumbest) mistake in Alaska business history. No doubt starving the *Daily News* throughout the JOA felt like victory to the *Times*; in reality, what it did was create resentment and desperation in a person they never should have riled: *Daily News* publisher Kay Fanning. Backed into a corner, she was forced to seek assistance, and she found more of it than Robert Atwood could have imagined.

Under terms of the JOA, the *Times* held its foot on the throat of the *Daily News* and never let up. Even a modest good-faith effort at sharing its now-guaranteed profits would have kept the *News* in permanent subjugation, its operations constrained by however much the *Times* permitted it to grow. The *News* by then was down to a staff one Outside journalist described as "Kay Fanning and her 12 disciples," had only twenty percent of the *Times'* circulation and no more Sunday paper. Apparently that wasn't enough for the *Times*.

It took five years and a federal lawsuit to adjudicate divorce proceedings in that loveless marriage. In the meantime, the disciples in our small newsroom at the *Daily News* soldiered on.

Chapter Five

Becoming investigative

What kind of publisher would assign two of her eight reporters to work full-time on a speculative, blue-sky investigation that was unlikely to pan out? Who would decide her struggling number-two newspaper ought to investigate and provoke the most powerful institution in the state? Who'd believe a couple of young and largely inexperienced staffers in their twenties could root out corruption in the state's biggest, most feared labor union?

Well, it probably it helped if she had cut her teeth on Chicago politics and journalism. Lucky for us, Kay Fanning had.

Investigating Alaska Teamsters Local 959 over the summer of 1975 was Kay's idea. I wasn't present at the inception—the assignment naturally filtered down to me through editors—but I'm sure the idea was all hers. After all, Executive Editor Stan Abbott was responsible for getting the paper out six days a week and wasn't likely to have volunteered one-quarter of his reporting staff to chase wild geese.

Yet the idea seemed like a natural to Kay, I imagine. Though she came to her job as owner and publisher via marriage, not the newsroom, she'd been schooled in Chicago to expect that there would be corruption, and that a good newspaper was responsible for rooting it out. I can't say when or why she decided to focus on the Teamsters, but I had known for a while that she wanted us to dig deeper, and that I was expected to be a key digger.

Kay had been getting ready to go hunting for some time. In 1973 the paper, as poor as it was, had sent me to New York, where the American Press Institute was holding a new training program for investigative reporters. In the midst of the unfolding Watergate investigation in Washington, twenty or so of us gathered at Columbia University for a two-week series of lectures and workshops that ranged from moral theory to practical use of the Freedom of Information Act.

Typical of newspaper institutions at the time, as much learning took place in barrooms as at the seminar. The organized program likewise was inspirational and instructive.

Bob Greene told us about *Newsday*'s now-legendary Heroin Trail investigation. A couple of *Miami Herald* reporters had to leave the seminar for a while to help track down Cubans involved in the Watergate burglary. David Burnham of the *New York Times* talked about his police corruption stories that sparked widespread reform and became the basis of the movie *Serpico*.

I was especially taken by Burnham, who started his talk by telling us "a good investigative reporter needs a low threshold of moral indignation." After his presentation I followed him out of the seminar, onto the subway, and all the way to his doorstep in Brooklyn Heights—asking questions all the way.

I believed he smiled at me with some bemusement when I mentioned that I thought the billion-dollar Trans-Alaska Pipeline Project might be a good place to look for corruption. He allowed as how it probably would.

I was not quite twenty-three. Two weeks of seminars and barroom conversation about uncovering voter fraud and police corruption left me vibrating with expectation; I didn't want to leave New York, but I couldn't wait to get home and get started.

It didn't take long.

I continued to cover stories every day like everybody on our small staff, but also managed to carve out a role for investigations.

Tips from inside state government in Juneau led me to a story revealing favoritism in the award of architectural and design contracts.

Elaine Warren and I wrote extensively about the troubles of a city manager on the Kenai Peninsula and I later pushed that story farther by reporting investigators' belief that a prosecuting attorney had tailored his presentation to the grand jury to minimize any charges in the case.

I was learning all the time. The state official in charge of the biased contract awards was a bellicose, burly former construction manager; he scared the shit out of me every time we met to go over my discoveries, but I learned to bluff my way through. Simple, really: never let them see you sweat.

Dealing with the prosecutor whose work my stories questioned likewise held a lesson. I called him at home one evening to set up a "confrontation interview" for the next day and thought I was ready for what I expected to be an angry and emotional response.

What I got was far more upsetting. Instead of the tough assistant district attorney, the telephone was answered by a little girl. When I asked to speak to the DA, the little girl put down the phone down and yelled "Daaaaady" several times. All at once my target became a human being—somebody's husband, somebody's son, somebody's daddy. I couldn't help thinking what it would mean to them if I wrote the story I had planned, and I weighed my responsibilities in a new light.

Yes, I wrote the story anyhow. What he did was deserved to be made public, and that wasn't my fault. Leaving the story unwritten could have had consequences for other people's spouses, dads, and daughters, including people who might not find justice in a corrupted system.

It was a clear call in the end, but still painful. His daughter's lilting call for "daddy" changed my calculus in such circumstances forever. I promised myself I'd remember that feeling every time I wrote stories that would damage reputations—and I would write a lot of them before I was through. As an editor I would share that anecdote with generations of reporters whenever they seemed a little too gleeful about their triumphs.

I learned another valuable lesson from an even tougher teacher: fear.

In the course of investigating the story behind a double murder at a trans-Alaska pipeline supply warehouse near Fairbanks, a state trooper source had given me copies of an intelligence report on two Arizonans believed to be in Anchorage to scout the potential for big criminal profits made possible by pipeline construction.

The document was only mildly interesting until I got to the last page, where Salvatore Spinelli and Jerome Max Pasley both were identified by law enforcement as "known associates" of the Bonanno organized crime family in Arizona. There were some notes of names, dates, and incidents—a license plate spotted at a Bonanno wedding, that sort of thing.

I started poking around, checking the usual court records and property liens and the like. I also conducted some unconventional research, including snatching two big bags of garbage in the middle of the night from the curbside at one of their houses. I learned a great deal about how to sort frozen garbage in a small apartment, but found little of value.

A few months after my midnight garbage run, I got up early one morning, bought a large coffee at the convenience store on the corner, and drove back to Spinelli and Pasley's neighborhood on a new mission. No more Mister Garbage. Today I was playing Sneaky Gumshoe.

I never had tailed anybody before, but I'd watched a lot of movies and TV shows where people did. How hard could it be? My plan was to spend the day shadowing the Arizona partners. I didn't know what to expect, but wasn't that the whole point of investigating—learning something you didn't know?

My prospects looked bright at first. I parked in an alley in my yellow VW bug and smoked while watching Pasley's house. I wished I'd brought binoculars. I wished I'd eaten something. And I had to pee, too.

My pulse raced a little when a large black sedan backed out of Pasley's garage a few minutes later and pulled away down the street heading away from me. Perfect.

I pulled out seconds later but slowed down quickly. Couldn't get too close, after all. My VW was still slimed with mud from breakup, that delightful season in Anchorage when the winter snows finally melt, creating acres of mud and revealing a winter's accumulation of slowly thawing dog shit. Still, my car was bright yellow where it showed through, and VWs weren't that common in Anchorage then. Belatedly I wished that I had thought to borrow a more average-looking car.

Oh, well. Too late now.

Their big car drove purposefully out Gamble Street and onto the Seward Highway, heading south out of town. They kept going past International Airport Road, already at the edge of the city. They keep moving until the last junky building along the highway disappeared and the view down Turnagain Arm opened up before us. The contrast between that vista—the narrow fjord ringed with steep, snowy mountains—and the trashy stores and bars on the outskirts of town could hardly have been greater. It was like lifting the lid on a dumpster and finding yourself in the middle of a park.

Surely, these guys weren't going all the way to the ski resort at Alyeska, or all the way to Seward? There was just one highway out of Anchorage to the north and this one to the south, so their choice of destinations was limited. I watched with relief as they turned off suddenly onto a small frontage road I recognized; it led to an old shooting range along the mudflats by the ocean there.

"Bingo," I thought to myself. I drove past their exit, turned around, and returned on a side road where I could look down at them on the shooting range. It was too far away to see them well, but they were both firing hand guns. One sounded like a .45 or .44 Magnum; for sure it was an automatic, bucking and barking several times in quick succession.

This was perfect. Not only would the scene make for great color in my next story—guns and gangsters went together naturally—but as I recalled one of them was on probation in Arizona. Playing bang-bang with handguns was nearly always a parole violation.

Soon enough the men put the pistols back into the trunk and drove away, heading toward town. I followed on the busy highway, no longer much concerned about losing them. I had my scoop.

When they turned into a shopping center on the outskirts of the city I almost kept going but instead pulled in behind them and drove to the far side of the parking lot. I backed into an open space and watched them drive through the lot, apparently looking for parking—except they kept getting closer, driving slowly down the lanes but always advancing toward me. My heart started pounding now; they were headed right at me, no doubt about it.

Anxiety turned into cold fear when the car pulled directly in front of my parking space and stopped, blocking me in. The passenger's electric window lowered slowly to reveal Jerry Pasley, smoking a cigarette, wearing sunglasses and staring straight at me. Seconds passed, though they seemed like minutes at the time. He raised a hand to his mouth, took out the cigarette and flipped it, hard, between his thumb and middle finger.

It hit my windshield squarely and bounced off. His window closed and the car pulled slowly away.

I sat in stunned disbelief. My mind raced, but coherent thoughts wouldn't form. For a few seconds I'd actually expected to die, feeling the atavistic terror a rabbit must experience just before the wolf's jaws close. I wanted to cry like a schoolgirl, to run and hide, to find somebody bigger than them to protect me.

I was shaking and thought I might throw up. When I felt a little steadier I pulled away, looking everywhere for a lurking black sedan, constantly watching my rear-view mirrors. What the hell did I do now?

I was pretty sure they didn't know me. Probably they just wanted to scare me—mission accomplished—and they'd forget about me now. Why would they care if some local kid in a yellow VW bug was watching them? I told myself this over and over, but I didn't believe it for minute. Instinctively I headed for home, a ratty Spenard apartment in a former motel next to a liquor store. Impulsively, I walked straight to the bathroom and found an old razor, scraping my face in desperation, shaving off the beard I'd worn for years in the vague hope that a new look might disguise my identity.

Moments later the phone rang. I jumped at the noise and then answered.

"Ah, hello?"

"Why the FUCK are you following us around?" a loud voice demanded.

"What do you mean, following you?"

"Don't play games, you little prick. Who are you? What the FUCK are you doing?"

My mind was racing again. This time I actually thought of something.

"Listen, I don't want to talk about it on this phone," I said. "Can I come see you instead?"

"Huh." A pause. "Yeah, that might be smarter. You know where my club is, The Mining Company, right?"

"I can be there in an hour," I said.

"Be here, prick."

I'd bought myself an hour, but what now?

How had they found my phone number so fast? Only one answer, really: they had a friend somewhere, either the DMV or the cop shop, who could run the number of a license plate for them on a moment's notice. Jesus. These guys really were gangsters—gangsters with pistols.

I could think of nothing to do but go see them, though. If they had my phone number they also had my address. They hadn't asked who I was, but they probably knew that, too. If they had my name it wouldn't take long to connect me to the newspaper. I couldn't think of a way to dodge or weasel my way out of this one.

It was only a ten-minute drive to his nightclub so I had a few minutes to think. There wasn't much I could do, but I wanted to cover my ass somehow before I walked in there.

I called a friend from the newsroom and told him the unvarnished story. "Very, very stupid," he said. "What are you going to do?"

Have to go meet them, I told him. But I wanted somebody to know what I was doing ... just in case.

What the hell was I thinking? Why, why, why did I do this stuff? What's the payoff, really?

My face was red and sore from the hasty shave, but there was nothing to do about that now.

On the way to the bar I hatched a plan, the only one I could think of. It was bold, audacious, unpredictable.

I decided to tell them the truth.

There was nothing special about The Mining Company nightclub. The name made it sound like a tourist place but it wasn't. It was the latest in a succession of bars that had been going out of business in the same location in Eastchester Flats for as long as I could remember. In an earlier life it had been a club with strippers, and in a subsequent incarnation in the early days of disco somebody tried to import that dance trend to Anchorage. Hardly anybody in town owned a white suit, though, and the new club owner soon learned most Alaskans would rather drink than dance.

I saw an older guy alone at a corner table when I walked into the dim room out of the bright daylight. He didn't look at me. I took a few breaths while my eyes adjusted to the light and then walked over.

"I'm Howard Weaver," I said to Salvatore Spinelli.

"The fuck?" he said with a puzzled look. I stood still while he stared. I couldn't think of anything else to do. Finally he grunted and shook his head. "You're here, sit down," he said.

I wasn't even sitting yet when he leaned forward on his forearms and demanded accusingly, "Didn't you have a beard this morning? I saw you had a beard."

"It was, uh, fake. You know, like a disguise."

"Huh?"

He stared in silence for a few seconds. "What the fuck, Weaver? Why the fuck are you following us around?"

I stuck with my plan and told the truth. "I'm a newspaper reporter; probably you know that by now. I heard you guys were mobsters from Arizona and figured if I could get some big scoop on you, it would be good, you know, for my career."

He was silent and still. His face betrayed no emotion. In the silence, I felt compelled to say something else and I was just about to.

Then a short bark of laughter erupted and Spinelli's body shook as he tried to swallow it. A grin split his face and suddenly he was laughing again, mouth wide open. I sat in silence. He finally quieted down, looked up, and rubbed away some tears from his eyes.

Then he spoke in short staccato bursts, head shaking as he did. "Oh, fuck. Mobsters. Newspaper. Oh, fuck me," he said.

He settled back and looked at me again. "So you wanted some hot story about the mobsters, yeah? Something to sell some papers, make you into a big shot?"

I looked down at the table. "Something like that," I said.

"Jesus, Mary, and Joseph." He was quiet for a long moment. "I think you're telling me the truth, kid.

"You want something to drink, Howard Weaver?"

He waved and the listless bartender scurried over. I ordered a Tanqueray and Roses lime juice, not much ice.

I began to think this might work out. "I'm sorry for following you, for acting like a punk."

"At least you did the right thing coming here face to face and tellin' me the truth. Not everybody would have done that."

Drinks arrived and he was quiet again for a moment, and then said, "Tell you what. I accept your apology. Don't be a dumb ass no more, though. It's stupid following me around. You ain't gonna see nothing, and people don't like to be followed. You like to be followed, kid?"

"No sir," I said. Half the gin was in my stomach by now and I felt a little better. Calmer. Maybe I wasn't even going to get my ass kicked.

"Well, there it is." He slapped the table, rattling ice in the drinks. "You don't like it. I don't like it. Don't do it no more.

"From now on, you want to know something, you come here like this, face to face, and you ask me like a man, right? Any legitimate question, you get the answer right from me. That way, you always get the truth, yeah?"

"Okay, sure. I mean yes, I will. Ask you, I mean, if I need to. Sir."

"And you drink here when you want to." He waved at the bartender. "Remember, this kid drinks on me, yeah?

"Any legitimate question, kid. Any time. In fact, you ask me something right now. What do you want to know?"

What the hell was I supposed to do now? Asking anything actually sensitive could be disaster, blow this whole kiss-and-make-up deal. If I asked something phony or stupid, that might piss him off, too. I was starting to realize Salvatore Spinelli was a lot sharper than he looked.

"Well, one thing I'd like to know is this: how did you get my phone number so fast?"

His barking laugh echoed around the room again with that. "Oh, fuck me. I guess you are a newspaper guy after all.

"I ain't gonna tell you that. I said any LEGITIMATE question. That ain't what we call a legitimate question, understand?"

"Yes sir," I said. "I think I'm starting to understand."

•••

I didn't write about them at that time, but Spinelli and Pasley's big exposure came a couple of years later, when they earned mention as bit players in "The Arizona Project," a massive investigation into corruption and organized crime in Arizona. The ten-thousand-word series was the product of more than fifty investigative reporters from around the nation who went to the state after *Arizona Republic* staffer Don Bolles was lured to a meeting and killed by a car bomb while probing corruption in Phoenix. It ran in newspapers all over America.

The report confirmed the police intelligence reports I'd seen. Spinelli and Pasley surfaced on day sixteen of the series in this context: "Peter and Michael Licavoli are said by DEA to be financing smuggling rings. Peter, apparently the brains in the family, also ramrods a pipeline of drugs, prostitutes, and stolen goods between Tucson and Anchorage, Alaska. Operating in Alaska are two close Licavoli associates, Salvatore Spinelli and Jerry Max Pasley..."

The next day Spinelli rated a second mention in the series. In a story about competition in Arizona between mobsters connected to Chicago and New York, they reported, "On the other side of the street, Edward (Acey) Duci, a Joe Bonanno soldier, is probably the most vocal of the New York group mobsters. He is closely tied to Sal Spinelli of the Tucson Bonanno-Licavoli group. Duci's main racket is prostitution, and he also helps look out for Bonanno interest in Phoenix. He is openly disdainful of the Chicago faction ..."

Chapter Six
Pulitzer lightning

With not much more than those few investigations under my belt, I set out a few months later with partner Bob Porterfield to track bigger game in the state—Teamsters Union Local 959. I had this much going for me: if you're headed out, at age twenty-four, to investigate the most fearsome institution in Alaska, you definitely want to be alongside a guy like Bob.

It would hard to imagine a more complementary pairing than Bob and me. We were both young, but he was somewhat older and more experienced and had a pugnacious personality defined by boundless energy and suspicion without measure. Bob was pretty sure everybody was crooked.

Bob's cynicism balanced my idealism; my interviewing skills smoothed some of his rough edges. With only two of us assigned to the investigation at the time, each of us naturally did some of everything, but in general he became the documents wizard and I handled our more delicate sources. His skillful documentation provided the framework for the project while I worked to put context, color, and confirmation into the package.

This started as what journalists call a blue-sky investigation: no specific tips or leads to follow, just a general sense that something needed scrutiny. Thus we started out with basic research, simply trying to define the union everybody in Alaska talked about but almost nobody knew. We spent weeks poring over U.S. Bureau of Labor statistics and filings, lawsuits, business licenses, and property records; days sorting through overlapping boards of directors and lists of union officers and employees. In those pre-computer days we kept records on five-by-seven note cards. Each cross-reference meant making a tediously hand-copied duplicate. Bob was especially good with colored pencils, and soon we had covered poster boards with red-green-blue spider webs to illustrate relationships nobody in Alaska had ever connected before.

For instance, why was Jesse Carr, head of the state's biggest labor union and by nature an adversary of big business, also on the board of the state's biggest bank? Not such a big mystery, it turned out. Anchorage's ruling establishment was small and cohesive. The bank's owner and president happened to be the brother-in-law of Robert Atwood, whose *Anchorage Times* once ran an editorial suggesting the Teamsters chief would make a good candidate for governor.

We learned some nasty stuff about the union and its operations, cost an influential legislative staffer his job, and created some federal tax problems for a lobbyist, but I am most proud of our fundamental accomplishment: we gave dimension to something that had been shrouded. The union was big and powerful, but until our report revealed how big, and why powerful, its reputation for being ferocious exceeded the reality. Bob Dylan would describe this phenomenon years later on the album *Empire Burlesque* when he sang, "What looks large from a distance/ up close ain't never that big."

As it happens, a sharp contrast in approaches to journalism would emerge from this story. As we were nearing completion of our months-long reporting project, we started to hear about some other reporters traveling around Alaska to talk with many of our sources. They weren't from the *Anchorage Times*, but far worse: the *Los Angeles Times*.

For whatever reason, the newspaper had decided to make Alaska, the pipeline, and the Teamsters its own story and sent a team of reporters north to do so. We were terrified. Stacked up against the L.A. paper, our odds seemed hopeless. With a circulation then numbering more than a million and a news staff approaching 1,000, the paper had won eight Pulitzers and its voice boomed where ours strained to whisper.

We considered rushing into print with everything we had in hand, but resisted. We owed readers in Alaska the best and most careful report we could create. I'll admit I didn't feel good about our decision a month later when the first of their Alaska stories appeared under a full banner headline on the front page of the L.A. *Times*: "Crime Wave Strangles Alaska." That melodramatic tone continued into the opening paragraph, which began, "Widespread lawlessness, a helpless government, and the stranglehold of a single Teamsters Union chief severely threaten a state crucial to the nation's future energy independence."

Shit. I'd been reporting for months and I hadn't spotted any crime wave strangling Alaska.

When we made it into print three weeks later, our December 4 debut ran beneath an understated question mark headline: "Teamsters: how much power?" Our series logo described in general what we thought the answer was; we called it "EMPIRE: The Alaska Teamsters Story." True to form, our lead was far less dramatic than the Californians' and began this way:

"Teamsters Union Local 959 is fashioning an empire in Alaska, stretching across an ever-widening slice of life from the infant oil frontier to the heart of the state's major city.

"Secure under the unquestioned leadership of Secretary-Treasurer Jesse L. Carr, the empire has evolved in just eighteen years into a complex maze of political, economic and social power which towers above the rest of Alaska's labor movement—and challenges at times both mighty industry and state government itself."

What we reported was a lot more meaningful than the flashy anecdotes that populated the L.A. *Times* version. For example, simply exposing the union's intimidating style of negotiation helped strip it of some mystery. We reported that tossing the employer's contract offer into a wastebasket and kicking it across the room was a fairly standard Teamster tactic. Somebody—Kay

Fanning herself, I imagined—refused to allow us to use an even better anecdote about the time Jesse Carr rolled a contract into a ball and gave it back to management along with a jar of Vaseline. By demonstrating how pervasive Teamster representation and power had become, we gave actual shape to what had been looming suspicion. And by detailing the web of relationships Bob had traced with his colored pencils, we showed why this was no ordinary labor versus management fight.

Teamsters 959, one local covering the whole state, represented truck drivers and deliverymen, of course. It also represented firemen, school principals, bakers, meat cutters, draftsmen, illustrators, and the Anchorage Police department employees who didn't wear badges. Workers' calculus was simple and easy to understand. If you wanted to be represented by a union in Alaska, why would you choose any one but the best?

The return for members was, for a time, fantastic. Construction had been a leading industry in Alaska since World War II and it exploded with the coming of the trans-Alaska pipeline. With 23,000 union members working, Teamster trust funds were collecting one million dollars a month in employers' contributions and were depositing the money in the bank where union boss Jesse Carr served on the board. There was no equally reliable engine of cash anywhere else in the state.

The union provided a dazzling menu of benefits. The *Anchorage Times* politely described it as "cradle-to-grave" coverage. At the *News* we called it "womb to tomb," but the Teamsters themselves preferred "erection to resurrection."

Promising "freedom from foreseeable disaster," union protection started with health coverage including pre-natal care and a Teamster-owned hospital; prepaid dental and vision insurance; a recreation center whose pools and gyms rivaled the state's best private clubs; low-cost group vacations organized by the union; college scholarships and vocational training; and a credit union and prepaid legal funds.

There was also a death benefit. And, yes, the union also sent flowers to every member's funeral.

It seemed too good to be true, and ultimately it was. The union's largess couldn't last, having been made possible for a time only because the pipeline boom swelled the rolls of dues-payers and extracted extra concessions from employers desperate to get on with building the pipeline. The pipeline project was run on a "cost-plus" basis, which meant expenses would just be passed along up the next level, ultimately paid for by consumers at the gas pump. But that million-dollar-a-month gravy train couldn't last forever, as we pointed out in our analysis. And it didn't, as we reported a few years later when union finances collapsed.

The Teamsters' success came with big political and social costs. To win its privileged position in the state, the union trafficked in both crime and influence, employing at one point no fewer than fourteen former state cabinet or deputy cabinet officials and the state's most powerful lobbyist, himself a former commissioner of labor. That kind of influence paid multiple dividends, such as the lease that gave the union twenty acres of prime state-owned land at the edge of downtown for $350 a month.

Even more noteworthy were the thugs and felons we discovered working at North Star Terminals, a Teamster-controlled pipeline distribution warehouse in Fairbanks. Though owned and operated by a private firm, the warehouse actually was run by the Teamster hierarchy. The number one union official there was Fred Dominic Figone, known to Alaska law enforcement as "Freddy The Fix." His number three, Bernard House, had been convicted of first-degree murder but later was pardoned by a Republican governor. The union's number one "yard man" was Peter Rosario Buonmassa, another convicted murderer—in his case, one who had been pardoned by a Democratic governor. Teamster boss number four in the terminal was Jack Martin, who had been convicted of violating the Mann Act, commonly known as the White Slavery Law against interstate transportation of women for prostitution. About six months after our reporting, Martin's badly decomposing body would be found not far from a rural roadway near Fairbanks. He had been shot twice in the front of the head.

From these and other tales, we knew violence sometimes visited Teamster operations—and Teamster critics. The *L.A. Times* later said its reporters typically traveled in teams of two while in Alaska "partly as a matter of safety." Whatever. I never felt endangered, joking with Porterfield that sustaining a flesh wound during our investigation would cement our reputations for life. My VW bug burned to total loss in my driveway during our reporting, but this was far more likely the result of my mechanical neglect. Our public profile and visibility as reporters at a local paper offered some protection.

Any real courage involved Kay Fanning, who was playing You Bet Your Newspaper by intruding on Anchorage's tight and tidy ruling clique, a group with room for labor bosses and bank presidents, but none for a plainspoken lady newspaper owner. Not one businessman we interviewed who had dealt with the Teamsters would allow the use of his name, and there was a reason for that.

The Empire series ended in late December, 1975. By the end of January I was 600 miles away in Juneau where I comprised the newspaper's one-man capitol bureau, primarily covering the legislature. I was still there in May when Stan Abbott summoned me to Anchorage for a meeting to plan followups to the Teamsters stories. The *Daily News* spent money with great reluctance in those days, and this planning session didn't seem urgent to me, but I was happy to get away from rainy Juneau and spend a weekend with Barb Hodgin, the girlfriend I'd gotten serious about just before moving away in January. On Monday, May 5, I was in the paper's second-floor newsroom on Fifth Avenue as the workday began.

Those of us who'd worked most on the Teamster project— Abbott; Managing Editor Tom Gibboney; reporter Jim Babb; Porterfield and I—had just gathered in Kay's office when the putative planning session was interrupted by a phone call.

Kay listened for a few seconds and then held the phone away from her ear.

"It's the Associated Press in New York," she said. "We've just won the Pulitzer Prize."

Chapter Seven

Our own newspaper

I realized later that Kay knew about the prize beforehand. Her thoughtfulness in making sure I was in town for the announcement was completely in keeping with her classy behavior. Stan Abbott must have known as well, because champagne showed up in the newsroom almost before we finished hollering. To my lasting dismay, somebody on the staff had one of the empty bottles delivered to the *Times* newsroom across the alley later that morning. When you're winning there's no need to gloat or showboat.

My folks were both dead by then, so I called my grandparents in Texas to share the big news. It didn't seem to mean much to my grandfather, or perhaps he was just hard of hearing. "Poetry prize?" he asked. "What the hell are you doing up there, boy?" Grandma's reaction was more gratifying.

Kay bought lunch for everybody next door at the Hotel Captain Cook, and pretty much the next thing I can recall is being in the basement of Abbott's house at a higher-octane continuation of the celebration much later that evening. There hadn't been much time for reflection.

Within a day or two I was flying back to work in Juneau, where I was met at the airport by most of the capitol press corps and presented with a bottle of Teacher's Scotch, which I drank solely because I'd read somewhere that it was Jimmy Breslin's favorite. Walking in to the press table at the back of the House of Representatives later that day I was stunned by a standing ovation from the members.

Anybody's Pulitzer is special. This one, for us, was more. We'd won not just a Pulitzer, but *the* Pulitzer, a gold medal for public service. I believe the *Daily News* was the smallest paper ever to have done so; at twenty-five, I was amongst the youngest reporters. More important, it was the first Pulitzer ever won in our state, where an inherent inferiority complex born of many years first as a U.S. possession and later a territory before becoming the forty-ninth state, made any sort of Big Time Recognition the source of not just individual but community pride. I know the legislators who recognized my return to Juneau that day were applauding not mainly for me, or for the *Daily News*. They were proud to have a Pulitzer Prize in Alaska.

Well, me too.

It didn't change my work in Juneau, though. I hated it. Covering that legislative session remains the least satisfying newspaper assignment I have ever had.

Reporters sat at tables in the back of the legislative chambers only a few feet from the nearest legislator and certainly close enough to see what morons many of them were. Legislation reached the floor to be voted on by members who hadn't been to any of the committee hearings; I knew that, because I had. People voted on important bills they hadn't read; I knew that, too, because I had.

Back in Anchorage, it was easy to think about state government as an extension of the civics lessons you learned in high school. Up close, the smell made it hard to fool yourself.

The more I learned about legislators, state government, and what was happening to Alaska, the angrier it made me, yet I felt largely powerless. Journalists were objective, right? Just the facts, ma'am. I wrote a few stories that tried to poke through the public illusion of the legislature as a high-minded, public-spirited institution, but somewhere between the copy desk in Anchorage and my own constipated sense of fairness they often wound up being "he-said, she-said" stalemates at best. Looking back, I recall that while I was perpetually pissed about what I saw, my real anger centered on my feelings of impotence to do anything about it.

By 8 p.m. most days I'd finished my third or fourth superficial story of the day and transmitted it to Anchorage on a crude Telecopier fax (a Mojo wire of my own now, no more racing to the telegraph office). It didn't take five minutes to get from the capitol press room to the Latchstring Bar at the Baranof Hotel, and I rarely strayed from that straight path down the hill. From there it was only a few steps farther to the Triangle or the Red Dog, and by that point the steps had ceased to matter; I just went where that night's tide was running.

Most of those nights I spent with a handful of other reporters who shared my growing conviction that we'd never be able to tell the truth with a collection of he-said, she-said stories. Though my paper gave me more leeway than the wire services or the other dailies, it was still fundamentally constricting. This was a debate that would echo throughout my career and come to full flower with the blossoming of blogs and citizen journalists thirty years later.

I lived alone in a single room at the Bergmann Hotel with a bare light-bulb and shared bathroom down the hall, so there was little incentive to go "home" each night. A legislative aide with a similar room described the old Bergman as "like living in the streets, only drier," and we missed no opportunity to be elsewhere. When the State Convention and Visitors Bureau held a reception for legislators, for example, we were there, loading up on jumbo shrimp and cheap white wine. If the teachers union held a fundraiser for some senator, we were there, too, huddled in a corner waving for the girl with the king crab canapés to come around again.

From there we were back out on the tide, washing from bar to bar on Front Street.

Work, party, work. Repeat as necessary.

Thank God we were young and strong. In Juneau, every night was Friday night—but every dawn was Monday morning.

Frustration with our journalism was a common topic of conversation. Hunter Thompson's book, *Fear and Loathing in Las Vegas,* had just been published, and in Washington reporters not much older than we were shaking the foundations of the Nixon government. We, on the other hand, were busily quoting legislators saying things we knew weren't true about subjects on which they were vastly ignorant.

I was too deeply in thrall to the Church of Journalism at the time to violate the sacred creed of objectivity, even if my editors would have allowed me. The only answer, we decided in our barroom conversations, was to start a new kind of newspaper and make it clear from the beginning that we wouldn't be playing by those old rules.

Respected national journals did it; the *Nation,* the *New Republic* and the *National Review* all wrote about politics with a decided point of view. Elsewhere a different journalism ecosystem was struggling to find a foothold, an alternative or "underground" press born in the Vietnam era where you could say "fuck" in print and write as boldly as you dared.

I was likewise enraptured by the kind of narrative reporting collected in Tom Wolfe's 1973 book, *The New Journalism.* It celebrated not just freedom but style, bringing back a literary aesthetic American journalists had abandoned in their quest for empirical, bloodless, just-the-facts reporting. In that world journalists were also writers, using the techniques of novelists to craft compelling narratives that looked not just for facts but also The Truth.

Way beyond carnival sideshows like Hunter Thompson, practitioners such as Wolfe, Gay Talese, Joan Didion, Michael Herr, and Gail Sheehy were blazing stylish new trails I ached to follow.

The idea for a publication of our own was conceived in Juneau by AP reporter John Greely and me. John was at once a student and a fan of politics, the kind of rare reporter who relished and understood both policy debates and back-room knife fights. His prose was being suffocated by the AP Stylebook and a cadre of aged editors in Seattle who studied and applied it with Talmudic devotion.

John and I knew far more than we could tell and were looking for a way out.

We were untroubled by our ignorance about business practices or sales. John was working for a non-profit cooperative, and I was employed at a money-losing newspaper, so neither of us was well schooled on the finer points of publishing economics. Actually, we hadn't been schooled at all. Instead we substituted an abiding faith in the "if we build it they will come" model that has motivated dreamers everywhere.

In addition to our confidence in the power of unvarnished truth-telling, we convinced ourselves that we had discovered a niche, an unmet need that we could occupy profitably while we told the truth and raised hell. No other media in Alaska provided statewide coverage.

Alaska was, and still is, mostly a state in name only; the legislature was one of the only places that even pretended to a statewide perspective, and even there the fundamental differences between an Eskimo finance chairman from the Yukon delta and a white speaker of the house from Anchorage were stark.

Cocksure of our journalistic capacity and ignorantly confident in our business plan, we would allow the idea to gestate for months, but we were already pregnant.

Chapter Eight
Encore for a Pulitzer

When you win a Pulitzer at twenty-five, many people think it's cute to ask, "What will you do for an encore?" The real shitheads ask, "What's it feel like to know you've already done the best work of your career?" I heard both way too often.

For the *Daily News* as an institution, the glow of the famous prize was eclipsed quickly by the gloom of its crumbling finances.

I returned from Juneau when the legislature adjourned in June, itching to try our new journalism plan, but unsure how to begin. When Stan Abbott called me in to say I wouldn't be getting the full percentage salary increase I'd heard others mention, my first response was to be a smart ass. "What do I need to do for a full raise?" I asked friends. "Win a Nobel Prize?"

I felt bad almost immediately and even worse when I learned a few days later that the paper was broke and perhaps just weeks away from bankruptcy. Giving me any raise at all in those circumstances was a classy move.

The paper had always lost money and been subsidized by something. I'd long heard the original owners survived by making enough money printing the Anchorage phone book to cover expenses at the paper. Kay had taken over with a sizable bankroll of her own and later had assistance from her son Ted Field, an heir to the fortune of one of the richest men in America. His father,

Kay's former husband, was Marshall Field IV. Kay had tapped her own sources as deeply as she could and Ted's as deeply as he was willing.

Kay determinedly searched for answers amongst rich friends, potential local partners and fellow newspaper owners nationwide. No doubt the sunny optimism characteristic of her Christian Science faith sustained her in hearing "no" over and over again.

Meanwhile, news of the paper's dire straits became public. Concerned Anchorage readers quickly formed the Committee for Two Newspapers and started going door to door to sell subscriptions. Kay tried without success to renegotiate the rotten deal she'd been forced to swallow earlier in the joint operating agreement with the *Times*.

It was soon clear that much of the newspaper's already-diminished staff would be let go. I wasn't in the management loop but I'd heard enough to expect big layoffs. Rather than wait, I announced that I was quitting to start a weekly newspaper. I don't recall anybody laughing directly in my face.

Two other young *Daily News* employees left to join John Greely (then 28) and me (I was almost 26): reporter Andy Williams, 33, and my younger brother Mark Weaver, 23, then the paper's librarian and general gofer. Andy, like Greely and me, had covered the legislature, bought into the idea of a statewide publication, and was willing to move to Fairbanks. Mark would become our production manager. The four of us contributed $1,250 each—yes, just $5,000 total—to capitalize the company. Soon we were joined by Rodger Painter, 29, John's AP colleague from Juneau.

In October, five months after winning the biggest award in journalism, the *Daily News* laid off five of its ten reporters. More would have lost their jobs had the three of us not left on our own.

We worked for the next several months in a friend's remodeled garage designing a paper and planning coverage. Along the way we settled on a name: *Alaska Advocate*. (I'd proposed "Alaska Advocate & World Defender," but lost the argument). Selecting the name "advocate" was intentional, meant to signal that we wouldn't pretend to be neutral or nonpartisan in the traditional journalistic sense. I also lost the argument over a corporate name, which came to be Visible Inc. My suggestion would have made our intentions even plainer: Sword of God Publishing.

By leaving John in Juneau and sending Andy north to Fairbanks, we immediately became the only news organization in Alaska with reporters in each of the state's three largest cities. We leased a telex line and installed tickers in all three offices.

Of course we needed more money. Barb Hodgin and I were living together by then, with brother Mark as a boarder, and she had both a paying job and a love of journalism. (And, it would turn out, of me.) After our first date at a drive-in movie, we'd gone down to the *Daily News* to watch the press run after midnight. The only continuing financial contribution I could make to the *Advocate* was working without a salary, as some colleagues and I did for the next three years. Only Barb's idealism, generosity, and affection made the adventure possible for me.

In his Alaska book, *Going to Extremes*, Joe McGinniss quoted me talking about *Advocate* finances: "Next we might try a sale of unregistered stock. Can you believe it? Twenty-five years old, with a Pulitzer Prize in my pocket, and I'm going to wind up in prison for stock fraud." Not long after that I bought the fanciest blank stock certificates in the stationery store and had an embosser made so we could "issue stock" to backers. Barb nearly cornered the market; I stayed out of jail.

The vast majority of people we asked about money lacked Barb's enthusiasm for our plan. My family had always banked at First National Bank (a small account, I assure you) so I took our business plan in hand and naively went to visit Dan Cuddy, the owner and president of the bank. He was friendly enough and listened to my practiced pitch and then said no.

"Do you know what a banker is, Howard?" he asked while showing me to the door. "He's a man who gives you an umbrella when the sun shines and takes it away when it rains."

As I remember it was Greely who came up with the idea of pre-selling subscriptions to raise money. We settled on the price based on nothing more than a notion of what we thought our friends might pay: twenty-five dollars a year. We printed a four-page flyer explaining what we were up to and starting asking. In three months we sold $10,000 in subscriptions to a publication that didn't yet exist.

This was a Kickstarter project almost thirty-five years before the internet's online pledge system for "crowdfunding" made its debut.

Chapter Nine

The virtues of excess

Early in my career the *Daily News* served as both playpen and training wheels for my journalistic infancy, but the *Alaska Advocate* was the real trial by fire that tested my emerging ideas about news. The lessons we learned there later gave us a crucial edge in the Alaska newspaper war.

For one thing, we learned that practicing journalism without much money isn't impossible as long as your girlfriend has a job. Almost nobody on the editorial side got paid (freelancers did, once in a while) but with housing and groceries paid for by supportive friends, lovers, and spouses, we could look for ways to stretch the few dollars we did have far enough to cover the paper's essentials: rent, printing and an occasional night out.

In addition to buying a little of our worthless stock, Paul Goodrich (a friend's father who long remained my guru) had given us a room full of government-surplus desks and chairs. Reporters generally came equipped with their own typewriters, so a few ashtrays and a coffee pot were all the additional furnishings we needed.

You did have to type on something, of course, and we soon discovered a cost-effective source of copy paper: the backs of the countless press releases and government notices we received. We were especially partial to releases from the Hickel for Governor campaign since it used high-quality paper and often hand-delivered the releases, which left them without bothersome fold marks.

I suppose we'd leased the teletype machines mostly because having them made us feel like a real newsroom. As a veteran of his one-man AP bureau, Greely had become a master teletype operator; Williams was also a wire-service veteran and comfortable using the machines.

Greely's copy always arrived clean and before deadline; Williams', not so much. In the capitol press room during my *ADN* stint in Juneau, I'd watched John type a couple of paragraphs onto the paper punch tape that actually fed the teletype beast and then start transmitting, able to both compose stories and type fast enough to stay ahead of it. The teletypes printed only IN ALL CAPS and included a bell that sometimes interrupted the intoxicating clatter to signal the impending arrival of an important message.

Likewise telephones were an essential tool, and in a state as big as Alaska that could mean startlingly expensive long-distance charges. We figured out early on that we could avoid many of those by calling out-of-town bureaucrats on their lunch hour; they'd usually return the calls later at state expense.

Advocate journalists were predictable attendees at any reception or press conference that promised free food—and, when we were lucky, booze. Foraging was a skill we'd all perfected working in Juneau, where every trade association lobby and publicly funded institution in the state showed up sooner or later to woo legislators with lavish buffets. In Juneau, alcohol was pretty much guaranteed at any event that started after lunch, and sometimes before. Anchorage events were less liquid and served more pedestrian hors d'oeuvres, but we made do.

When we moved our office into an old downtown Anchorage residence at 527 L Street—our fourth location in a little more than three years —my brother and our circulation manager Jim Erickson moved into the unfinished basement to save money. The result of our experiences trying to install plumbing for them turned out too disgusting to relate. On another occasion, Jim recalled a party where Mark's hockey buddies had grown rowdy and knocked over the big box filled with thousands of color-coded index cards that organized our subscription files. "In the computer language of today, it would be known as a memory dump," he recalled years later.

It would be fair to characterize much of the behavior at that office as Animal House with better drugs and fewer togas—except, of course, for devotion to our High and Noble Calling. We took the journalism very seriously, but little else.

The *Advocate* was a work-in-progress for its whole existence, as indeed it was meant to be. We were young, naive, angry, idealistic, ignorant, and tireless. We'd embraced an ad hoc consensus style of decision-making, though I emerged as de facto editor on account of being the founder who happened to be in Anchorage, where production, printing and distribution were centered. I also had ideas and wasn't shy about articulating them.

A year or so into our adventure, the enterprise seemed to me to be drifting away from our original intentions, too often covering the kinds of routine stories we'd promised to abandon for a higher calling. I responded with a twelve-page manifesto—grandly titled *Quo Vadis?*—addressed to fellow staffers. It reflected in large measure what we all aspired to:

"This newspaper ... has become too goddamned respectable. We have somehow lost track of the original spirit with which it was launched. We're trying to be all things to all people, to offer 'responsible' coverage and find a blend of contents that will satisfy some kind of 'general readership.'

"That's nonsense ... If we reduce the *Advocate* to some kind of mythical common denominator, we're spitting in the faces of those 'educated, active, and influential readers' we talk so much about. We're also saying something pretty degrading about ourselves.

"So, fuck the average reader; he doesn't exist anyhow, and if he does let him read the *Times*. We're doing something more important and exciting at the *Advocate*....

"When pressed, we often revert to the formulas that produced exactly the kinds of newspapers we are all running away from:

Keep yourself out of the story. Balance criticism with a favorable quote. Be objective. Two sides to every story …

"From here on out, let's pull out the stops. If we err, let it be on the side of excess. If we are irresponsible, let's be irresponsible to something besides our consciences.…"

I ended the manifesto by shamelessly quoting myself from the statement of purpose we'd published just a year earlier in the *Advocate*'s inaugural issue:

"We do not intend ever to view ourselves as part of the establishment. Too often, newspapers confuse their role with that of an official government process. They become weighted down with chains of artificial respectability and become just another cautious, sterile institution."

We tried to make our intentions clear. Early on we seized on a motto suggested by a *Daily News* colleague, Steve Kline, and attributed variously to everybody from Mark Twain to Abbie Hoffman: Sacred Cows Make the Best Hamburger. We wanted to class it up a bit, so photog and art director Ken Roberts, a seminarian in his younger days, dusted off his Latin for a rough translation: *Sacre Boves Optimus Hamburgerus Fiant*. Close enough.

Though we aspired to the narrative style of Tom Wolfe and fuel-injected energy of Hunter Thompson, our standards for accuracy and fairness were as mainstream and tough as anywhere I have ever worked. The work held up, too, winning dozens of Alaska Press Club awards alongside some national and regional recognition. (We cockily demanded that the press club allow us to compete in the category with the state's bigger dailies, where we kicked their asses.)

Greely's political and government reporting always demonstrated what combining extensive knowledge with our wide-open style of storytelling could do. In a rambling piece we remembered as "the gut-shot rhino," he chronicled the boisterous, pre-adjournment madness of a legislative session, employing a dozen observations and anecdotes copy editors would have trimmed from stories in daily papers or a wire report. His free-wheeling account included insights traditional journalism would have missed or omitted and ended with this telling quote from Governor Jay Hammond: "Somebody better take charge or the whole thing will collapse like a gut-shot rhino in a cloud of dust in mid-June."

Steve Cowper, a powerful legislator during our heyday and later governor of Alaska, told a reporter ten years later that the *Advocate* produced "the best political journalism that has ever come out of the state. They understood that the chemistry of politics goes beyond bill-making."

Rodger Painter carried the flag on another journalistic adventure: the time we simulated blowing up the trans-Alaska pipeline.

In June 1977, about five months after our launch and just after the *Times* ran a banner headline based on an idiotic oil-industry claim that the pipeline was safe from sabotage, we sent Painter and Roberts out to find out for themselves. What they did was simply drive to the town of Glennallen, where the pipeline and one of Alaska's few highways intersected, walk up to the pipe, and set off a smoke grenade. Red smoke curled skyward while they waited, but nobody responded. Our guys came home and told the tale in grand style. Law enforcement agreed the story had demonstrated vulnerabilities; oil executives and their establishment buddies frothed about how irresponsible we were. I think they should have thanked us for debunking the absurd claim and alerting readers to a real, though unlikely danger.

Not all our best work was that flamboyant. A personal favorite was a careful, brutally revealing examination of plans being advanced for a natural gas pipeline written by former college professor and freelancer Richard Fineberg. That article later won a major national prize—the Leob Award for business writing, which included a trip to New York for the ceremony and a $5,000 check. Richard, a banjo-playing railroad buff, flew as far as Seattle but then hopped freights from there to New York and back. He told me he kept the check in his shoe for safekeeping on the return leg.

Winning a national prize for business reporting was especially sweet; "anti-business" was one of the labels most often applied to the *Advocate* by critics. We had that reputation starting with our first issue, a package of stories detailing the dominance and abusive behavior of the *Anchorage Times*.

We were sometimes asked later on if starting off by disrespecting one of the state's most powerful institutions had been a good idea. I joked at the time that we had to write about Atwood in the first issue since we weren't sure there was going to be a second one.

Honestly, though, it was inevitable. We'd been motivated to start the *Advocate* as much as anything else by the *Times*' dishonest journalism and the fact that its only competition, the *Anchorage Daily News*, seemed soon destined for bankruptcy.

All our concerns were reflected in the headline across our first cover: Bob Atwood and the Media Monopoly Game.

Along with a catalog of the paper's abusive journalism, we zeroed in on what would become the *Advocate's* other persistent theme: the intertwining of the oil industry with the state's business and political elites. The *Times* and the industry were more than just connected; they were joined at the wallet. A sizable chunk of Atwood's fortune sprang from oil leases on the Kenai Peninsula, where he and a group of influential businessmen in Anchorage had been steered to profitable leases by insider information.

Thus we managed in our inaugural issue to alienate the *Times*, its chamber of commerce audience, and the industry that was quickly emerging as the state's most important. A number of Alaska's biggest companies bought ads in our first issue but never advertised again.

Andy Williams' take, quoted in a magazine article about the *Advocate* years later, probably had it right "If we hadn't blown it then," he said, "we would have blown it somewhere down the line. I think advertisers would have been alienated sooner or later anyway."

Our thinking about the paper's business plan—so far as it had one—was based on being Alaska's only genuinely statewide medium and on attracting influential readers. Smarter businessmen probably could have predicted that most statewide business institutions—in banking, telecommunications, airlines—were run by Robert Atwood's bosom buddies; many of the influential readers we had hoped to reach were his best pals.

Still, the *Advocate* did win readers across the state. They remained more important to us than advertisers—in our hearts, always, but also in our ledgers. At one low moment we offered a "lifetime subscription" for $100, as I recall; only later did subscribers realize that meant the paper's lifetime, not theirs. (In truth, though, I never heard a complaint).

At our peak, shortly before folding, the *Advocate* sold about 6,000 copies weekly from subscriptions and newsstand sales. At that point the *Daily News* was claiming 10,000 subscribers but probably had considerably fewer. It wasn't at all clear at that time which of us would survive.

We sent shameless fundraising appeals to everybody we could think of. Many small donations resulted, but only a single big one: one of our appeals had been passed along by its recipient to a New York philanthropist, William Ferry. None of us had never even heard his name, and the first and only time we heard from him was when his check for $10,000 arrived in the mail.

We also held fund-raising events, including a screening of *Citizen Kane* and a benefit concert by Doctor Schultz, the area's most popular rock and roll band. Thus we added "working capital" to keep the lights on and the presses rolling.

It cost about $1,000 per issue to print our sixteen- to twenty-page tabloid. There was only one printer in Anchorage that could do the work, and the politically conservative proprietor charged us the same rate that he charged a one-time customer, demanding cash in advance for every printing. Somehow we always came up with the money.

I once complained that we were regular, cash customers and shouldn't pay the same as people who walked in off the street for one job. The printer thought that over and said, "You're right. I'll start charging them more."

Terry Bailey, who held down the thankless job of bookkeeper during much of our existence, met with me weekly to decide which bills we could afford to pay. Generally we tried to pay individuals in need first, small business creditors second, and big companies last. "We knew if they were hungry or if they hadn't paid the rent or if they had medical problems," she told a Juneau reporter ten years later. "It wasn't a commune, but it was a very trusting situation around there."

We operated a typesetting service on the side that did occasional work for ad agencies, politicians, and others who needed camera-ready copy. That made money for us and my little brother did marry Jeanette Humphrey, the pretty typesetter.

It made some sense that the journalists who'd started (and owned) the *Advocate* were willing to work for free, but it was astonishing to me how much commitment others brought to the operation. Though we paid our typesetter, bookkeeper, and sales staff what we could, any one of them could have made considerably more money elsewhere. What's more, talented and equally committed staffers kept coming to work for nothing throughout our existence.

Photographer Roberts signed on even before our first edition, recognizing (as I did not) that we'd need more photo and art direction assistance than I'd planned. He immediately became indispensible. We decided to use a magazine-style, poster cover for our tabloid, and Ken created it more than a hundred times, always on a tight deadline. Staff members, friends, and even their children were pressed into service as models for imaginatively staged photo-illustrations that gave the paper a unique look and instant recognition.

Kay Brown, then the best reporter at the *Anchorage Times*, jumped ship for the *Advocate* in the early days and produced a series of in-depth reports on subjects ranging from questionable cancer cures to land-use planning. (She went on to become a five-term Alaska legislator and director of the Alaska Division of Oil and Gas, one of the state's most powerful agencies.) When she left the paper, her journalist-spouse Pat Dougherty stepped in, quickly becoming an essential editor and beginning the most valued professional relationship of my career. As he later remembered coming to the *Advocate*, "My first impression was, 'These people need help.' It wasn't particularly well organized, and graphically it was pretty primitive." Fair enough.

Neither Kay nor Pat got paid; both kicked in some of their savings when they came aboard.

Clifford John Groh, a local boy and whip-smart recent Harvard grad, likewise bought a small ownership share when he came aboard; school teacher and freelancer Satch Carlson did one of the toughest jobs in journalism better than anybody I've ever worked with, writing a consistently engaging humor column. Other regular contributors would include a symphony conductor, college professors, and a thoracic surgeon who described himself as "a human plumber."

John McKay, then as now Alaska's preeminent media and First Amendment lawyer, was generous with time and counsel, inaugurating a relationship that lasted through all my Alaska journalism career. In all my years in Alaska journalism I don't recall losing on any substantive legal issue when John was our lawyer.

Throughout the paper's existence, capital remained elusive. At the end of one of many memos proposing a new funding scheme to the staff, I wrote, "I am through crying wolf. This time either he gets me or I nail his fucking hide to the wall."

Looking back I'm reminded again that we had all the talent we could use. If only we had made some money.

Chapter Ten

Music in the cafes at night

Much of my generation's youth was spent in a kind of extended masturbation: we did things that felt good at the time but produced no lasting results. Our declarations about ending war and sexism, saving the planet, and changing things forever look pale and jejune to me now.

But some of what we tried worked, and some of it mattered. To me, Alaska mattered, and the *Alaska Advocate* made a difference.

Looking now at the state in its post-Palin phase, it's hard to imagine the political climate of the 1970s, an era in which a cadre of progressive young Democrats controlled the legislature and allied with a progressive Republican governor to adopt strict environmental regulations, raise oil taxes, and enshrine a constitutionally protected savings account that has since accumulated almost $40 billion in reserves even while distributing $18.4 billion in dividends to Alaska residents.

Alaska politics always comes down to debate over resource development—mainly about oil. The adversaries in the argument in those days were evenly matched and the body politic was a hormonal adolescent, undergoing great changes and still coming to grips with what it wanted to be. The decade in which Bob Dylan sang "there was music in the cafes at night and revolution in the air" was a heady, optimistic time to come of age in Alaska.

The razor's edge on which the outcomes of such battles balanced was demonstrated in the Republican gubernatorial primary of 1978, when pro-development candidate Walter Hickel lost to environmentally progressive Jay Hammond by ninety-eight votes. (Alaska has a tradition of such cliffhangers; in 1966 Hickel was elected governor with an edge of just 1,008 votes, and in 1974 Hammond won by a 287-vote margin).

However, when Hammond eventually was declared the winner, Hickel sued, enlisting the help of his former attorney general Edgar Paul Boyko to argue that widespread and ruinous mistakes by state election workers should invalidate the results.

As the case wound its way to the Alaska Supreme Court, the *Times* did its best to trumpet Hickel's cause. Every allegation of voting irregularity, every hint that Hickel might run a write-in campaign if he lost in court, was given a 96-point headline in the state's largest newspaper.

VOTE AUDITS DON'T JIBE, one *Times* banner proclaimed, falsely equating the official state audit with one done internally by Hickel campaign staff. OFFICES TO BE SEARCHED screamed another, hanging the story on another Hickel campaign claim. Still another *Times* story reported ominously about discovery of "a brown paper bag with some possibly questionable ballots." In fact, the bag was simply sitting just outside the room where Alaska State Troopers were guarding all the ballots. Those in the bag already had been tallied.

In waded the *Advocate*. In a series of stories over August, September, and October, we reported in detail on the allegations of election irregularities and the court arguments, especially important because Hickel, Boyko, and the *Times* continually discredited Hammond's win in the court of public opinion even before the legal arguments were over.

In the heat of the growing debate, I tried to spell out just why those tactics were wrong:

"There is no kinder word for it: the tactics employed by Edgar Paul Boyko in support of his election challenge are filled with the dangerous demagoguery Americans know as McCarthyism.

"It's a serious charge to raise against a respected public servant and officer of the court; it's a sad realization to come to about a man I have always counted as a friend.

"But the facts in this case bear no other conclusion."

Few were aware that Ed Boyko owned the modest old house on L Street that the *Advocate* was then using as offices—and, for some, dormitory. He was a good, fair landlord, and that didn't change after I wrote about him.

As a weekly, the *Advocate* had the advantage of examining the tense legal fight between Hickel and Hammond with a bit more perspective than many daily reporters could muster. We also had an edge in talent and experience. I had covered Hickel and Boyko for years; Greely was by far Alaska's best political reporter and had written about Governor Hammond when Hammond was a legislator and senate president; staffer Clifford John Groh grew up in Anchorage and was well-connected in the Alaska legal community; and an investigative bulldog named Bill Lazarus, who later became a lawyer himself, served as a one-man truth squad for claims and counter-claims as they emerged in court. All contributed to coverage of the case as it finally emerged from the Supreme Court in a legal victory for Hammond, who was elected governor that fall despite Hickel's vain attempt to win as a write-in candidate.

That outcome mattered. Over the next four years of his second term, Hammond gave his blessing to a federal bill setting aside eighty million acres of national land in parks and refuges; championed the Alaska Permanent Fund dividend as a way to protect the account that now manages $40 billion in oil revenues politicians otherwise would have surely spent; opposed a wide range of scatter-brain ideas, from carving a new capital city out of the wilderness north of Anchorage to handing out free state land to would-be settlers. Much of that would have ended far differently if Hickel had been elected governor.

I don't know that the *Advocate* ever articulated a position on journalistic objectivity, but we didn't have to. Frustration with journalism's rituals of detachment, balance, and disinterest had been prime motivations for the weekly's founding. It's no accident that most of us involved in the startup had been political and legislative reporters; there's probably no arena in which the distance between what reporters know and what they tell is greater.

I didn't feel objective. I cared about all kinds of things: journalistic things, naturally, like truth and openness and fair play, but also public policy, things like environmental protection and equality under law and getting a fair return for the riches the oil companies were pumping out of Alaska.

Somebody asked me when we started the paper, "What will you be biased about?" I decided to answer in a brief statement of purpose that ran on our opinion page:

"We are against all lies, and their more vicious stepchildren, the half-truths. We are against shadow in the conduct of public business, secure in our belief that there is no public affair best handled in the dark. We are against that which is dull or stifling. We oppose any limit or barrier to the exercise of talent. We believe that in the honest, unimpeded exchange of ideas the best course is to be found. We believe we can play a part in that process."

In a subsequent column I tried to spell it out another way: "We will resemble, on balance, more the guerrilla soldier than the regimented Redcoat. We see ourselves not as part of the organized system but as an alternative to it. We will be civilization's cheerleader and society's scold."

As a native son I felt particularly protective about exploitation of Alaska by what we called "Outside interests." (By Alaska journalistic convention, the O in Outside is always capitalized when used to mean "anywhere that's not Alaska.") Since the first Western contact, Alaska served mainly as a resource colony for whatever nation controlled it; the indispensable Alaska historian Stephen Haycox later would make that case authoritatively in *Alaska: an American Colony.* The Russians came, killed every fur seal they could find, and then abandoned the place. After the U.S. purchase came the gold rush, attracting tens of thousands of naive boomers to the north. When the easy gold played out after a few years those exploiters, like the Russian furriers, packed up and went home without worrying what they left behind.

Salmon was next on the exploitation agenda and, to a lesser degree, timber. In all cases Alaska's natural resources were plundered on behalf of rich owners thousands of miles away with little or no regard for sustainability or the damage done during extraction. Alaskans' desire to control development of their natural resource became a leading impetus behind the movement for statehood and self-determination. Particular passion arose over use of fish traps that scooped up every returning salmon in nets stretched all the way across stream mouths, a practice that led to precipitous declines in salmon stocks in the first half of the Twentieth Century. Banning fish traps was one of the new state's first actions; since then, local management has sustained the healthiest wild salmon industry in the world, perhaps Alaska's greatest sustainable resource success story.

I knew this history of Outside domination well and it seemed obvious to me that the same pattern was destined to repeat itself following discovery of the massive oilfields surrounding Prudhoe Bay. Their development raised two issues that dominated all others: environmental protection and fair taxation. In each fight, the basic split was between interests seeking the cheapest, quickest exploitation (and thus the highest profits) and those who took a longer view. Despite the bogeyman constantly thrown up by the oil industry and its friends, there was no meaningful "environmental extremist" or lock-it-up opposition to development in Alaska. The central debates weren't over "yes or no" issues but about how fast and furiously drilling could happen, and how much of the value the state would retain from lease sales and taxes.

I started writing about that theme almost from the *Advocate*'s first issue. This is from February 1977:

Alaskans must work and eat and so there will be development. Thinking people do not believe that will or ought to be stopped.

But the growing fear in the soul of Alaska is that such decisions will be orchestrated far away, by those with an eye only to the profits and products, with no feeling for the life we choose. As the wealth we shelter becomes more dear, the price we must pay for our values becomes immense.

The pressure is on, and growing. If there is something worth fighting for, prepare to start now.

At the time, I wrote most of my stories and columns on a metal, muddy-green Olympia typewriter decorated with quotations, such as John Donne's admonition to "observe the physician with the same diligence as he the disease." (That's good advice for any journalist.) Another was more overtly political: a weathered bumper sticker with the legend SECEDE OR SUCCUMB emblazoned against the Big Dipper symbol from Alaska's flag.

I didn't actually believe Alaska should leave the union; on a lot of issues that mattered to me, federal policy in those days was often more enlightened and balanced than local interests. But I did think Alaska should take greater control over its economic future, and that meant taking responsibility for oil development. It was a feeling widely shared at the *Advocate*, and by readers who turned to us for information.

After the *Daily News'* Pulitzer in 1976, an ad hoc "Hippie Caucus" of young legislators and their aides had presented me with a mock proclamation, complete with multiple "whereas" and "therefore" clauses, that described me as "a simple tundra boy." I took great pride in that.

As I would throughout my career, I wrote tirelessly about Alaskans' propensity to roll over for the promise of a quick, easy payday from Big Oil. I was especially infuriated by the slick public relations campaigns the industry employed—a relatively new phenomenon in Alaska's unsophisticated political culture. It seemed to me they were parlaying a few donations to the food bank and an orchestrated chorus chanting "jobs" into one of the sweetest deals they'd found anywhere on earth.

Alaskans were being played for suckers. Again.

I remember being particularly insulted by a 1977 Arco television commercial I described as "The Oil Boom Boutique Blues."

The woman, who looks like a natural for the Petroleum Wives Club, stands at the cash register next to a little boy who could be anybody's little league champion.

... this is the basic pitch: 'When Arco first sent us up here umpteen years ago, this was a real hole. Nothing to do, nothing to buy. Now, thanks to oil companies, there are boutiques and everything.

At this point she spins halfway around to display a pretty new outfit. The sales clerk, eyes glazed in delight, delivers the punch line: 'I guess this is what oil impact is all about.

Horse puckie.

... This [commercial] says to us that our life was worthless before oil came and brought the fruits of the good life to this backwater burg ... That is a lie. It is the lie that has been force fed to Alaskans ever since the big puddle of oil at Prudhoe Bay was discovered; the lie that is the real foundation of the trans-Alaska pipeline, the off-shore platforms and the mirror-windowed headquarters buildings in Anchorage.

Doesn't anybody else remember that this was a good place to live BEFORE oil? This was a land of promise long before the discovery of fossil fuels beneath the ground...

We will never live in a 'before oil' time again, of course. Even if Alaskans were not hungry for the quick fix of dollars oil development brings, we would be unable to slow the energy greed that compels other states to want our oil despite our concerns.

Since we cannot stop the development of our oil, we can at least make sure that it pays us well. Perhaps we can, by asserting our rights as landlords here, dim the companies' flashing arrogance a shade or so.

I also wrote in those early days about predictions I hoped would never come true—but which, tragically, did.

In May 1978—eleven years before the *Exxon Valdez* was crashed into Bligh Reef and poured the largest crude oil spill ever in North America into Prince William Sound—I watched with foreboding as the *Amoco Cadiz* spilled its crude off the coast of France.

This was not a rusty-bottomed, vintage Liberian tanker ... It was instead an American-registered supertanker, a world class rig much like those commissioned to transport Alaska's pipeline bounty southward from Valdez...

Alaskans are well advised to listen carefully to the lessons of Normandy, for there has seldom been a clearer parallel for us to observe...

Those who carry oil will spill it. And, since there is no apparent way to slack the world's thirst for oil, I suppose it will always be carried from wherever it is found to wherever it is sold. There is a sad ring of inevitability to all that...

Don't you see? The only variable is time. Alaskans are not waiting to see IF a major tanker spill will strike; the only question is WHEN...

If we can do nothing else, we can at least recognize that hard fact. As we watch oil company advertisements advise us of their concern for Alaska, we can remember their concern for France. And when it is time to tax them for the wealth they export, we can take full measure of the costs they will certainly visit on us.

Oil companies and their Alaska allies didn't like the *Advocate*'s coverage or that kind of commentary, and there were surely a few smiles in their tall office towers when we announced, in March 1979, that we were folding.

Chapter Eleven
Learning fast at the end

The *Advocate* folded far more quickly than it was launched. We made the decision to quit over one weekend, a long and emotional gathering of perhaps two-thirds of the staff in the living room of the house where I had grown up in Muldoon. What began as yet another parlay about how to sustain the paper had ended with the realization that we couldn't.

I called Greely and others who were out of town to check our decision with them; Greely quickly flew to Anchorage and earnestly explored whether there was anything else to be done. In the end, however, our consensus was unanimous. (Mark Hamilton, the talented general manager who had only just signed on to help, was out of town and I couldn't reach him. He learned of our decision when it became public, and I still feel badly about that.)

There were lots of reasons for our decision. While circulation continued to grow, advertising remained scarce. I honestly don't remember the numbers, but an independent story by Juneau freelancer Bruce Scandling published on the tenth anniversary of the paper's demise reported that we'd earned $153,000 in the first nine months of 1979 but incurred expenses of $180,000, even though we still weren't paying most reporters. By then many of us had been working two and a half years without pay (thanks,

Barbara); the previous year my total taxable income was the same number as my street address—228 dollars.

Our relentless 115-week marathon, while exhilarating, was also exhausting. No internet startup would ever work harder. As Painter wrote at the end, "The *Advocate* has been an extended family, demanding mistress, journalistic mission, political statement, artistic release, professional proving ground, and search for the Holy Grail all rolled into one."

On top of all that, the *Daily News* had just been sold to a big California company named McClatchy, and we were hearing about the paper's plans for expansion, promotion, discounted ad sales and the like. "When the elephants fought, we knew we were going to be stepped on" Groh said later. (During the subsequent war with the *Times*, readers often asked me if I thought Anchorage could support two newspapers. I always reminded them that I was the guy who once thought it could support three.)

News of our decision to fold soon became public. I just had time to write a short explanation for the paper dated March 8, 1979, our penultimate issue:

"[W]e kept coming to one inescapable conclusion: you can't get there from here... like every other community, there's a limit to [our] individual patience, effort and energy, as well.

"Many of us have been running with this long shot for better than 800 days now, and that's a long pull when it's all uphill. Nobody at the *Advocate*, as far as I can tell, feels cheated by the experience—the rewards have been great, if not always tangible— but everybody needs time to catch his breath...

"We'll have a lot more to say next week. For now, to a lot of folks out there (you know who you are), thanks. And to a few of the rest, up yours."

The next week's cover simply said "Farewell" in big type. Roberts had talked me into posing in mid-stride with a jacket slung over one shoulder, waving goodbye.

The last words in the last column I wrote for the *Advocate* came from Ernest Hemingway. Unfortunately I attributed them to the wrong book; the line actually comes from *For Whom the Bell Tolls*, not *Islands in the Stream*.

Nonetheless, the sentiment described my feelings precisely: "Christ, I was learning fast there at the end."

This iconic photo of Anchorage, Alaska perfectly reflects what I remember as the view looking east down Fourth Avenue as a boy. The photo was clearly taken before March 1964 when the Good Friday Earthquake destroyed much of the block on the left side of the street shown here.

Larry and Kay Fanning inspect a copy of the *Anchorage Daily News* fresh from the press shortly after their purchase of the paper in 1967. The paper's printing equipment was ancient even then.

A. Cameron Edmonson, left, was perhaps the oldest staffer when I joined the *Anchorage Daily News* in 1972 and Elaine Warren and I among the youngest.

Stan Abbott, shown here in 1974, guided the *Anchorage Daily News* with sophistication and style unusual for a small paper in those days. His sense of design and interest in unconventional, deeply reported stories helped shape the paper for decades following his departure in the early 1980s.

I started working at the *Anchorage Daily News* as a fifteen-year old high school junior in 1967 and joined the staff full-time within weeks of college graduation in May 1972. This photo was made about then.

I scurried after every assignment early in my career, which included coverage of brief refueling stopovers by U.S. government officials returning from Asia. Here, UPI's Helen Thomas, left, and Henry Kissinger were probably joking around while I took careful notes. In my youthful imagination I always pegged the unidentified guy in the hat as CIA.

One of those official stopovers brought President Richard Nixon to Anchorage. Just before he boarded Air Force One, someone handed him a copy of the *Anchorage Daily News* in time for this departure photo. Stan Abbott added the circle to make sure we didn't miss it.

On May 5, 1976, the day the *Daily News* won its first Pulitzer Prize, I'm standing with my partner Bob Porterfield, reporter Jim Babb, and Publisher Kay Fanning. Only a few months later, about one-third of the news staff would be laid off amidst warnings of impending bankruptcy.

Just after learning we'd won the 1976 Pulitzer Prize for Public Service, I called my new girlfriend, Barbara Hodgin (far right), with the news. She worked nearby and thankfully showed up in the newsroom to celebrate. Kay Fanning is on the phone at left, as is Stan Abbott (seated). Reporter Jim Babb stands by the window and Jeanne Abbott stands to my left.

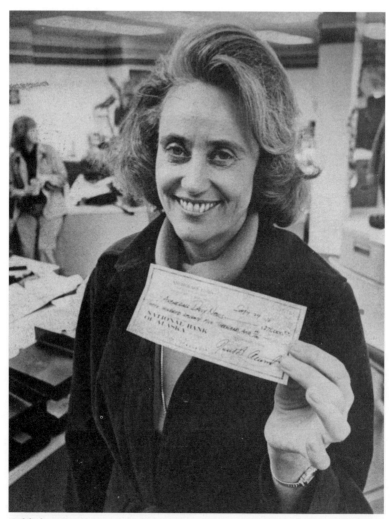

Publisher Kay Fanning holds a $375,000 check signed by *Anchorage Times* Publisher and owner Robert Atwood. It represented half of what Atwood paid to settle a lawsuit over the *Times'* treatment of the *Daily News* in a joint operating agreement under which the two papers operated from 1974-1979. Though Atwood settled out of court, Fanning was given only six months to rebuild a newspaper operation from scratch. That imperative sent her looking for help, and she found it in Sacramento, California when she approached C.K. McClatchy.

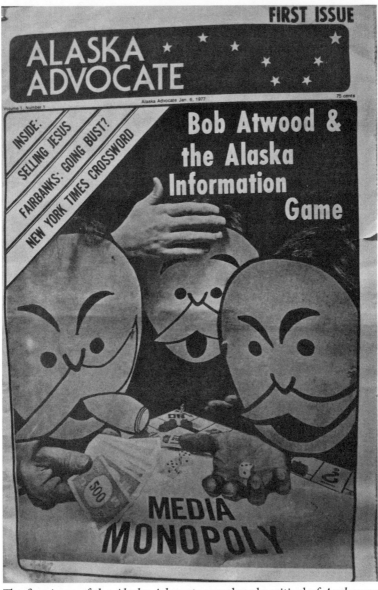

The first issue of the *Alaska Advocate* was sharply critical of *Anchorage Times* Publisher Robert Atwood, by far the most powerful media figure in Alaska and one of the state's most influential citizens. That article probably guaranteed the lack of mainstream advertising for the remainder of our 118-week run.

This somewhat filigreed image was the basis of a Christmas card we sent to *Advocate* friends and supporters one year and is one of the few staff photos that have survived the years. Back row, from left, are Mark Sutherlin, Jeannette Humphrey, Sherry Murray, Brad Stockwell, Mark Weaver, Mark Hamilton, Karen Lew and Ken Roberts. Front row, from left, are Diana Doyle (kneeling) Jolene Hildigard, John Greely, Eileen Herring, the author, Jim Erickson, and Bill Lazarus (kneeling).

The *Advocate* moved its main office in Anchorage office three times in two and one-half years of operation, starting in a converted garage and finishing in a comfortable old residence. The living room was converted into this newsroom with other offices and work spaces scattered throughout. Two staffers lived in the unfinished basement for a while to save money.

John Greely and I dreamed up the idea of starting a statewide weekly paper while we were covering the Alaska Legislature in 1976. Trained as an AP correspondent, Greely's gift for stylish and insightful political coverage found room to blossom in the *Advocate,* headlining what one governor would describe as "the best political journalism that has ever come out of the state."

Few *Advocate* photos ever showed Ken Roberts, for the simple reason that he took almost all of them. After a busy stint documenting trans-Alaska pipeline construction and its impact on the state, he volunteered to fill a job I hadn't realized we needed: photographer and art director. He designed and produced more than one hundred covers for the magazine-style tabloid.

Rodger Painter, who joined the *Advocate* in its early days, and Clifford John Groh, who became a reporter after offering to sell ads to get his foot in the door, were editorial mainstays through much of the paper's existence. This park-bench portrait was taken just before the paper folded. Cliff is holding a bottle of Prinz Brau beer, a local brew whose existence from 1976-1979 almost exactly paralleled that of the *Advocate.*

My new girlfriend, Barb Hodgin (now my wife of almost thirty-five years), enticed me to take some time off for a ten-day rafting trip down the Yukon River, igniting a passion that would carry us and rafting companions across the state in coming decades. Upon our return, I managed to turn the trip into a cover story, titled "Adrift With the Ghosts of the Gold Rush."

Chapter Twelve
A bugle, then the cavalry

The *Advocate* folded just as the new McClatchy *ADN* emerged, and nearly everybody on the weekly's staff who wanted to work on the daily was hired. The *News* needed reporters, and the pool of decent newspaper journalists in Alaska was small. I believe I'm the only one who had to get through an interview with the new owner before getting a job.

C.K. McClatchy told me later he needed to see whether I was "the big bomb-thrower" he'd been warned about. It took one three-hour conversation for him to decide I was worth the risk and for me to develop an affection and admiration for him that would only grow deeper over time.

We met at the Hotel Captain Cook, the city's best. At least I felt at home; not so long before I had been employed there, over three college summers, as a dishwasher, salad-maker, and ultimately night maintenance man. C.K. was accompanied by a friend, a suave San Francisco lawyer and politico named Bill Coblentz, and we sat in an alcove on the top floor, coincidentally overlooking the headquarters of the *Anchorage Times*.

C.K. never mentioned a job that day and I never asked about working for him. Instead he asked questions about Anchorage and Alaska, focusing particularly on personalities. He wanted to know how politics and government really worked in Anchorage—or at least he wanted to know if I knew. I had well-developed and deeply informed opinions about all that, of course, and three hours passed quickly and enjoyably while we chatted.

We parted cordially, still without direct mention of my prospects. A day or two later, Stan Abbott called from the *News* to tell me I was back on board at the paper, writing editorials.

Under terms of the JOA lawsuit settlement with the *Times*, the *Daily News* had until the end of March to establish its own completely independent operation. What that meant was pretty much starting a newspaper from scratch.

Because the *Times* had handled all sales, manufacturing, and distribution during the joint operation, all the *News* had left was its shrunken news staff. It needed an office building, a printing plant, a circulation department, and sales staff. It needed them all yesterday. It took a lot of money to arrange that, but money alone couldn't have done it. It also required expertise.

The McClatchy Company supplied both, buying a million-dollar building south of town and shipping up crews of printers, circulation executives, and editors from its California papers. Somehow a working semblance of a newspaper was patched together in the new building in an industrial park on Potter Drive and at the end of March we were ready to pull the plug at the *Times*.

Fortunately, April 1 was a Sunday, when we didn't yet publish a paper, so the "new *Daily News*" didn't have to debut on April Fool's Day. When it did appear on Monday it was a vastly different paper than the emaciated edition produced two days before on the final day of the *Times* agreement.

From two sections averaging perhaps 16 pages, the paper expanded to 48 pages—four sections of 12 pages each. Because ads were so scarce, the newshole—the percentage of space devoted to editorial copy—was huge. We practically shoveled copy through the new computer system to the production department to fill the unaccustomed space. In addition to hiring staff, McClatchy also had purchased an impressive array of news services, and we were able to offer Anchorage readers a broader choice of premium national and international news than ever before, supplementing AP coverage with stories and features from the likes of the *New York Times*, *Washington Post* and *Los Angeles Times*.

Within weeks, the circulation department was receiving a hundred new subscription orders every day. This did not necessarily mean a hundred new subscriptions were actually being delivered, recorded properly, or billed, however, owing to the stress and disorganization that defined our operations at the time. But things kept getting better.

Reliable delivery and prominent, well-stocked news racks became a prime directive. Any employee could earn a cash bonus simply by calling the circulation department to report an empty or malfunctioning newsstand; the "Rack Attack," we called it. Within months, the paper was selling more than 20,000 copies on some days, up from fewer than 10,000 in the grim final days of the old regime. *Anchorage Times* executives, displaying a fatal blindness that would contribute greatly to their ultimate demise, refused to believe those numbers.

Despite its overworked and understaffed departments, the paper looked good, already brighter and better designed than the stodgy *Times*—and, most important, arriving on doorsteps with increasing accuracy and consistency every morning. The *Times* arrived at mid-afternoon.

Thus began a pattern that would persist over the next thirteen years: steady progress and improvement at the *News*, stubborn denial at the *Times* and an inexorable reversal of the readership gap between the papers.

The folks who had been in charge while the *Daily News* declined—Kay Fanning and her executive editor, Stan Abbott—still presided, though their circumstances could not have been more different. The new owners pumped in resources for the battle—dollars, bodies, tons of newsprint, and barrels of ink. More important, they introduced a different attitude; where Fanning's operation during the JOA had been focused on survival, this incarnation intended to win.

Much of that change would manifest itself slowly over time, the result of incremental staff expansion, more efficient systems, and years of sophisticated strategic planning. But part of it happened overnight, with the arrival of a brash young general manager named Jerry Grilly.

One of my first recollections of Jerry involves a conversation in which he referred to our boss Kay Fanning, as "mom," which struck me as unbelievably cheeky. I was 29 and he was in his early 30s; Kay, then in her early 50s, was old enough to be our mother, I suppose, but after knowing her for ten years I still called her Mrs. Fanning.

Who was this guy?

I quickly learned, and often observed afterward, that part of Jerry's game was to push the boundaries as far as possible as early as possible in any encounter to carve out space for himself. It might wrong-foot an opponent who'd never encountered the like before, or perhaps charm a new acquaintance who couldn't believe he'd just a met a guy who seemed to say and do what everybody else only thought. In either case, it typically shifted the encounter into Jerry's court immediately, and he took off from there.

Of Jerry's essential contribution to the *Daily News*' unlikely victory, we can say this absolutely: if he had not existed, we'd have needed to invent him. No one person gets all the credit for the victory, but Jerry deserves a large share.

When Grilly arrived in Anchorage there was little reason to believe the *Daily News* would survive, and no reason at all to think it could win. With McClatchy's financial backing and strategic focus—both essential to our campaign—we knew there would be a window of opportunity, but the odds of us achieving more than tenuous survival remained vanishingly small.

To be honest, only a few people at the paper honestly believed we could win. Nobody else in Anchorage thought so, either.

Did Grilly really believe? I'm convinced he would have signed on anyhow, just for the fight, but I also think his boundless self-confidence convinced him it could be done. His first job was to persuade people at the paper that it was possible. Then he had to make believers out of key people in town.

Doing so required a blend of salesmanship and swagger that few people ever muster.

Grilly was a tough, street-smart kid from Cleveland, a Vietnam veteran with an enormous appetite for self-promotion who swept up everything around him. He moved—and expected those around him to move—at "the fastest speed known to man." Because he believed so completely in himself, he believed in the cause he was championing. Such was the strength of his conviction that before long, a lot of other people believed, too.

He could not have been more different from the tailored, graying, well-bred lady he worked for, Kay Fanning. She was religious, polite, and well-mannered. He was profane, pushy and ill-tempered. She was abstinent; outside the office, he was often drunk. ("When somebody asks if I want to go have a couple of drinks, I tell them no. If you want to go have ten or a dozen, I'm your guy," he once told me. I understood.) She was tightly wrapped; he was undisciplined. Gambling with him once in Reno I watched him hand his Visa card to a cashier for more chips, whispering to me, "One time soon they're going to just keep this fucker and cut it to pieces."

I never asked either Kay or Jerry about how their relationship worked.

Jerry was the Wild Colonial Boy even while Kay was still around. When she departed in 1983 to edit the *Christian Science Monitor* in Boston, he was left essentially unchecked and managed to shift into an even higher gear. At one point in our adventures he took to calling me "Mad Dog." In choosing a suitable nickname for him in response, I decided "Death Wish" was the most honest.

Jerry was simply outrageous. I'll admit that I was, too, but believe me: he was way more outrageous. I can mount no better defense on our behalf than the explanation George W. Bush once offered: When we were young and foolish, we were young and foolish. It was often a great deal of fun.

Jerry and I spent many nights in topless bars and bottomless bottles, broke some laws, and dodged some bullets. It's useful to consider our behavior in context—Anchorage was itself a little young and foolish in those days—but the truth is that we were pushing against and occasionally past the edge.

Although we could happily play and party together—and we did—day to day work life could still be problematic. Despite the many virtues Jerry brought to the newspaper war—confidence, determination, imagination—there were some nasty behaviors, as well.

He could be a bully; more than once I watched him publicly thrash subordinates from the business side of the paper, sometimes reducing them to tears in department-head meetings. He tried it only once with me; I employed the approach I'd learned as an investigative reporter and pushed back instead of blinking. It never happened in front of other people again.

A number of people told me of occasions when they believed Jerry double-crossed them or worked behind their backs, and some people told me there were times when he did that to me. Maybe so; it didn't register much with me. What I remember is that during the times I was most vulnerable, Jerry always stood behind me.

He was also self-indulgent, missing important meetings to sleep in after his latest adventure or coming unprepared to meetings for which the rest of us had been frantically preparing. By the spring of 1992 questions about his performance and behavior reached the point that an important advertiser and business associate felt compelled to tell me about his concerns.

We met twice in one week: the first was a chance encounter at which he unloaded spontaneously for forty-five minutes, the second a lunch date a week later to follow up and talk more formally about his concerns. I'd seen some of Jerry's worrisome behaviors myself, and while I didn't mention any of that to the advertiser, it certainly made me listen to his criticisms more closely.

I decided not to do anything. I didn't tell anybody or pass the concerns up the chain of command. Jerry and I had been to the war together, and I decided this wasn't going to turn me against him. I also chose not to confront Grilly directly, a decision I now regret. Frankly, I didn't think it would do any good. It seemed certain the issue would come to a head some time, but those concerns were in the distant, uncertain future as we rolled out the new *Daily News* in 1979.

Chapter Thirteen
Bright and cheerful colors

Kay Fanning figured in my journalistic life from its early days, though at the beginning the lowest-ranking editor loomed larger in my world as a high-school stringer than did the publisher's wife. By the time I'd worked my way into a full-time job in the newsroom, however, her husband had died and she was both editor and publisher, and from that moment on she played a central role.

I arrived at the *Daily News* by way of Muldoon and East Anchorage High with ambitious intentions but a distinctly limited set of expectations. What Kay did for me, more than anything else, was to change them; simply by being who she was, she helped me become more than I would otherwise have been.

It's probably impossible for recent arrivals or strangers to the city to understand how close the horizons loomed in Anchorage in those days. It was a very much smaller town, insular in many ways, often more than a little narrow-minded. It may be that Kay's greatest and most lasting gift to Alaska was the way she changed the sense of possibilities there; I was one of many beneficiaries, and by the luck of the draw was close enough for long enough to get more than my share.

Look: Kay Fanning knew Mike Royko and had tea with Ann Landers. Newt Minnow was her lawyer. She'd eaten dinner at the

White House and been to opening nights at the Metropolitan Opera. I remember standing in her living room while I waited for her one day, taking down one book after another from the shelf and noticing that most were autographed, to Kay, from the authors.

I didn't know anybody else in Anchorage of whom those things were true, and neither did most other people.

If the folks at Wikipedia are ever looking for an illustration of "classy middle-aged woman, circa 1975," any photo of Kay Fanning would do fine. She seemed perpetually composed and self-assured. If she ever violated the never-let- 'em-see-you-sweat rule that I later embraced, I wasn't around to see it.

Kay simply couldn't see any reason why Anchorage ought to be backward; the common local phrases "good enough for Anchorage" or "just as nice as Seattle" didn't figure in her vocabulary. She knew there was something very special about the land and people of Alaska and she was determined to make sure we all lived up to that promise.

She went about that mission with a profound sense of respect that I came to appreciate only much later. In much the way people change their opinions about their parents, it would be fair to say that the more experience I got as a reporter and editor, the more I respected Kay. As a journalist I sometimes chaffed at what I thought of as hesitation or timidity. I learned to frame arguments not so much on facts and logic as appeals to her better nature. Though her society upbringing and religious practice as a devout Christian Scientist sometimes clashed with the mores of journalism on the frontier, her instincts and ideals were reliably on target. Nowadays I also recognize, in hindsight, how often she was right and I was wrong about some approach where we had differed. Only after her departure—and my own expanded responsibilities—did I fully understand or appreciate the blend of judgment and balance she displayed.

In much the same way, it took me years to realize how very brave she had been to assign me and Bob Porterfield to investigate the Teamsters Union. I had some romantic notions about personal danger in those days, but I had no appreciation for the size of the commitment she was making when she took on the state's most powerful institution. It is no exaggeration to say that nobody else in Alaska—no businessman or banker or politician—would have dared to do it. Indeed, none ever had.

That firm backbone came in an outwardly refined, sometimes almost prissy package. She'd given up drinking before moving to Alaska as a newly divorced young woman in 1965 and, after her second husband's death in 1971, didn't serve liquor in her home. For those of us more culturally attuned to Alaska's heritage, this made for some dull parties, though Editor Stan Abbott sometimes stocked a guest bathroom shelf with miniatures of Scotch that insiders knew where to find.

In her memoir, *Kay Fanning's Alaska Story*, Kay compellingly describes her expenditure of family fortunes to sustain the paper's tenuous finances and the constant worries that can't have been good for her husband's health, but her outlook always seemed sunny from where I sat. My wife Barbara spent some time one summer helping Kay plant the flower garden at her home, and she took away an insight I've remembered ever since. There was no room in that garden for anything purple or somber, Kay told Barbara—nothing but bright and cheerful colors.

One measure of Kay's affection for Alaska was the fact that after her retirement, she returned not only during summer (typical) but also spent some winter months visiting as well. That was only one small demonstration of how thoroughly she became an Alaskan. From her earliest days, Kay understood truths about the state some people never figure out. Far more than most, she understood the special circumstances of Alaska Natives in a land being engulfed by other cultures, and her paper championed better understanding before, during, and after her stewardship. Four special reporting projects from 1965-1990—each a remarkable achievement for its time—sought to bring understanding of Native cultures to urban residents: The Village People, The Emerging Village People, The Village People Revisited, and then A People in Peril.

Kay's agreement with McClatchy Newspapers was a rabbit-from-the-hat maneuver that resulted in a deal that surely ranks as one of journalism's least promising investments. McClatchy family friend and lawyer Bill Coblentz sat in on the discussions and always claimed that when he left for a bathroom break, Kay started crying and C.K. McClatchy added another million to his investment.

"Most expensive piss I ever took," Coblentz would grumble good naturedly later, always earning a laugh. I suppose the story might even be true.

McClatchy bought eighty percent of the *News* in that 1979 deal, leaving Kay and her family twenty percent. Much later I learned that she had planned to give Stan Abbott and me, and perhaps others, small shares from her portion, but McClatchy objected to further dividing the ownership. When Kay left in 1983 to edit the *Christian Science Monitor*, the first woman ever to edit a national paper, the company bought Kay's remaining shares and owned the *Daily News* entirely.

Chapter Fourteen

It wasn't an accident

After Kay moved to the *Christian Science Monitor* and Stan Abbott departed to work for McClatchy in Sacramento, I moved up to the top job in the newsroom. Our circulation—jump-started with discounted rates, contests, and giveaways—sustained its impressive growth, but advertising sales lagged far behind. For most readers, the *Daily News* remained an add-on; they already subscribed to the *Anchorage Times* and were taking us for a test drive. As a result, advertisers would gain only incremental exposure by placing an ad in both papers, and few did.

Some, like the large grocery-store chain that was the *Times'* biggest advertiser, wouldn't buy ads in the *Daily News* at all. Though the longtime Alaskans who owned the Carr's grocery chain were more philosophically aligned with the *News* than the *Times* (Larry Carr once ran for governor as a Democrat), the grocer's commercial and business interests cut the other direction. Perhaps there was an actual or unspoken blacklist against advertising in the upstart paper; certainly we thought so, though now I'll never know.

McClatchy's Erwin Potts later would reveal that the *Daily News* lost more money in the first month than the company had expected to lose the first year. Lucky for us, it was also growing faster than anybody could have hoped, and thus held greater promise. As it turns out, the company's CEO—reserved, soft spoken C.K.

McClatchy—shared the combative spirit his ancestor had displayed 122 years earlier in launching the company in California's rough-and-tumble gold rush. As the stakes grew higher, C.K. confidently pushed more chips to the center of the table without blinking.

No doubt the Alaska adventure was an absurd business risk, but C.K. believed it was possible to win—and that trying was absolutely the right thing to do. Alaskans deserved a better paper than the biased, boosterish *Anchorage Times*, and he was rapidly giving them a clear choice.

Times Publisher Robert Atwood later would say he had simply been unable to complete with the McClatchy's deeper pockets, but the truth is the *Times* didn't compete on any level. For instance, it stubbornly refused to acknowledge that most modern readers preferred to get their paper in the morning. Had the *Times* shifted early on to compete head to head in the morning, it might have smothered the *Daily News* in its crib.

His paper likewise clung to its identity as the voice of the Anchorage establishment. Its news coverage was deeply biased in favor of downtown commercial interests and for years it refused even to run letters to the editor critical of the paper or its friends.

The *Times* always believed itself to be a reflection of the true majority of Alaskans, but increasingly that wasn't true. Thousands of newcomers arrived each year from more sophisticated American cities and many expected more than a country broadsheet. The *Times'* blind spot—like their arrogance and entrenchment—hurt it in ways its owners couldn't even conceive.

But this was my generation coming of age in Alaska, not theirs, and I could feel the change winds blowing. Even as Alaskans began to awaken to the benefits of preserving some wilderness, the *Times* remained perfectly consistent in its strident, unilateral disapproval. Before statehood, Atwood testified to a Congressional committee that, "In Alaska conservation, as it is and has been practiced, is paralysis ... this so-called conservation is actually a waste of the worst sort." Many years later his paper was still describing an opponent as "an admitted environmentalist."

Nowhere was its bias as blatant as on matters of oil development. As the *Advocate*'s first issue illuminated, Atwood's cheer-
leading for the industry improved his personal finances. He was
called the "boomer extraordinaire, [who] daily preaches the gospel
of unlimited growth to the people of the last frontier" in *Lost
Frontier: The Marketing of Alaska*, an important book by Peter
Gruenstein and John Hanrahan. Neither they nor other research-
ers who tried could find a single example of the *Times* opposing
a significant development project, or endorsing any substantial
environmental initiative.

So the paper had some vulnerabilities: it published in the
afternoon; was increasingly out of sync with readers newly arrived
to Anchorage; its bias was increasingly transparent; and when it
wasn't campaigning for or against some special interest, its news
judgment was uniformly old fashioned and dull.

But those were small chinks in thick, apparently impenetrable
armor. C.K. and other McClatchy executives knew how difficult
winning in Alaska would be. The *Times* position was not simply
dominant; it was overwhelming. At the beginning of the fight its
circulation was greater than the next six largest newspapers in
Alaska combined. It published the only Sunday newspaper in the
state, the dowry the *Daily News* had been forced to turn over in
its shotgun marriage to the *Times*.

McClatchy's money and expertise helped boost the *Daily
News* immediately. We hired staff and added sections; in those
early days, as editorial page editor, I was responsible for a new
weekly "Perspectives" section.

However, despite our progress—bigger papers, more staff,
increasing circulation—the paper was in too many ways an
underachiever. In September 1980, I outlined my dissatisfaction
in a memo to Kay Fanning: "The *Daily News* is a good newspaper.
It's not a great one, and can't be without clear, consistent pressure
from leadership ... Working at the paper has often been viewed
more as a calling than a profession. Reporters felt lucky to work
here (What else was there in Alaska?) and management was

grateful that they would work long hours for low pay. That's an incestuous, corrupting relationship and it has led to considerable indulgence on all sides."

The memo outlined what I thought was wrong and how I'd go about fixing things. Though I honestly didn't intend it as such at the time, it proved to be my opening salvo in a campaign to take charge.

I started by lobbying for basics: higher standards ("Good people go when bad people stay," I wrote), more training, better pay, incentives. I promised to involve staff more in making decisions, a practice I'd amplify and employ throughout my career. "Reporters are by their nature bright, curious, and pushy. We treat ours like children ... This doesn't mean we let the staff run the place, but that we make sure they understand how and why decisions are made, and give them a chance to state their case."

"How can we accomplish all this?" I asked rhetorically in another memo. "I can do it for you."

A month later I sent a note that now reads like a cheeky ultimatum. My frustration with missed opportunities and stalled initiatives had boiled over. I wanted my hand on the rudder.

"A great newspaper doesn't come to be accidentally, or even because someone wishes it would. It can happen only as a result of continued, disciplined effort directed expressly at that goal ... We can't be an excellent newspaper without being profitable, but we could certainly be profitable without excellence ... I believe Anchorage and Alaska need a newspaper that will labor with intelligence, integrity and independence to tell the stories that need telling."

Apparently my message resonated. Not long afterward, Frank McCulloch, McClatchy's vice president for news, came to town for a periodic visit and invited me to lunch. Too dense to recognize this as a job interview, I was thrilled to spend time with the legendary newsman who had been managing editor of the L.A. *Times*, globetrotting foreign correspondent, and celebrated

Saigon bureau chief for *Time* magazine during the height of the Vietnam war—the kind of leader reporters talked about for years after he had moved on.

As I remember that lunch, we mainly talked about journalism: why we loved it, why it mattered, how it could be improved. At the end of the meal he asked straightforwardly if I thought I was ready to move up in management.

I'm embarrassed to remember my response. Yes, I told him, I thought I'd be a good editor. I wanted to help make the paper better and had a plan to do so—but I insisted that I wasn't ready to turn my back on reporting forever. "I'm really mostly a writer," I said. "I don't expect to end up in management."

He answered kindly, and framed the question again with the best insight I've ever heard about leadership.

You won't get to choose again, he cautioned. A good leader makes a clear promise to the people he leads: I'll be there for you, you tell them. You expect them to work hard, use all their talent, struggle to get better. In return you pledge to do everything you can to create and sustain an environment where that can happen. You get them all the money and tools you can. You take the heat from the politicians they piss off, you catch the flack from the publisher. In return, they follow you.

That's the deal, the fundamental transaction. "And you know what, Howard? Your account with the staff is never balanced. If you want to be a great leader, and I think you do, you'll never be able to walk away. There's no going back."

I had no idea then how profound and true his observation was, or how completely that unspoken bargain with staffers would rule the next decade of my life. But I knew for sure now that I wanted the job, and I believed I could do it.

I was getting the chance to put up or shut up much sooner than I imagined. I had just turned thirty and was about to be put in charge of the journalism in the *Daily News*.

Chapter Fifteen
The distant emperor

I realized even as it happened that the Alaska Newspaper War was a rare and special experience, though I was far too callow to know how profoundly that was true.

In the early days I liked nothing better than to talk about big ideas and rhapsodize about great accomplishments yet to come. It's impossible to estimate the number of hours I spent in barrooms talking about what was wrong and how to fix it, describing the grand things that could be done "if only..." It was certainly a very large number.

Suddenly I was in a position to do something more than talk about all that. To a growing degree, most of those "if only" conditions were now mine to determine.

I'm proud to recollect that the aspirations and determination that were to lead the *Daily News* to so many victories were present even in those first weeks and months of my tenure. I look back at old memos and journal entries and sometimes blush at my presumption, but never have to cringe over the ambitions. We often didn't know how to accomplish what we sought, we were sometimes wrong and occasionally lacked the talent, but we never lacked for the nerve to try.

In short order a Gang of Four had coalesced around the opportunity my appointment offered: alongside me stood Pat Dougherty, then as now my journalistic soul mate; Rosemary Shinohara, multi-talented and utterly dependable; and Mike Campbell, an intuitively skillful and stylish practitioner of newspaper creation.

As owner, Kay Fanning held the traditional title "editor and publisher," and so the top position in our newsroom always had been executive editor. I kept the title "managing editor" though I was editor in all but name, in charge of both news and opinion pages. I had never liked the sound of "executive editor;" I didn't get into news to become an executive, after all. Besides, at the moment it was counter-productive to change my title anyhow. For one thing, if I wasn't called managing editor I'd be expected to name one, right? I wasn't ready.

Thus, perhaps unknowingly, we established the kind of "flat hierarchy" favored by the management gurus we'd never heard of. I named my three lieutenants "assistant managing editor," "deputy managing editor," and "associate managing editor," defying anybody to craft an organization chart reflecting relative position.

Each had authority drawn straight from me and each could get things done in any corner of the newsroom. I had a little office in the corner; nobody else had one at all, and I swear I don't know to this day whether the door to my office would close. We were aligned by instinct, inspiration, and desire; the foundation we shared was aspiration—a hunger to do something extraordinary.

A reasonable (if unlikely) goal for us would have been to work for stability and financial survival. A greater and more noble intention would have been to upset the *Anchorage Times* and become Alaska's largest newspaper. But what we really wanted was to be the best newspaper in America, and there wasn't anybody there to tell us we couldn't try.

By the time our wildly unpredictable run was over, we had accomplished the first two and sometimes brushed up against the third. On reflection, I am convinced that one of the things that made it possible was the absence of limits imposed from outside.

We were a little newspaper 2,000 miles north of the mother-ship, far from anything resembling micromanagement. Our paper didn't even arrive in the executive suite in Sacramento until days after publication, delivered by mail. McClatchy was a small company with a hard-won tradition of local autonomy. As a result, when people asked me if we could try something I'd often answer: "Why not? The mountains are tall, and the emperor is far away."

To their lasting credit, when the McClatchy brass heard about our audacious motto, they embraced it with laughter and pride.

On any list of reasons about why we were able to pull away from our larger, well-established opponent, I'd put that one first: we were allowed to experiment, fail, and learn. Good ideas had a chance to fight it out with bad ideas, and the good ones usually won. When we did screw up, we'd get up and try again, educated and fortified by what we'd learned in failing.

Of course, we had to earn our relative independence. The paper was doing well and in newspapers as pretty much everything else, nothing succeeds like success. The quality of the paper was improving, the number of prizes won was mounting and—far more important—our circulation was growing.

Really growing. If the *Anchorage Times* had taken a clear-eyed look at the evidence of our growth back in the early 1980s, its managers would have sounded the klaxon and sent all hands to battle stations. But they didn't. Instead they insisted that we were lying about the numbers, that we were giving away the paper and ads (some truth to the latter), and that they hadn't felt any impact at all.

Thus the second entry on my list of suggestions about pulling off a long-shot victory: find yourself a stupid opponent.

Their foolishness would be demonstrated in many ways over the next decade, but they all boiled down to pretty much the same point: The *Times'* owners and managers were drinking their own bath water, so smug and satisfied with themselves that they allowed us to tunnel under them until their foundations finally collapsed. By then it was too late to respond.

Reason number three: our emperor, although distant, was one tough mother.

Maybe this is a good place for me to pause and acknowledge that yes, I do understand newsrooms alone do not win newspaper wars. No doubt arguments over advertising pricing policy and circulation fulfillment strategies were every bit as fierce and colorful as our pow-wows in the newsroom — but I am not writing about them. I'll simply once again express my profound appreciation and admiration for what the folks on our business side accomplished. Their feats are worth a book of their own, and I hope they get one.

McClatchy's corporate support was the singular ingredient without which none of this could have happened. Of course their dollars were necessary, but their strategic acumen and cold-blooded nerve were likewise fundamental.

"McClatchy's support" at this point, meant more than McClatchy Newspapers, as the company was then called. We also enjoyed the personal support of C.K. McClatchy himself, the man whose role at the head of the company bearing his name meant he could push more chips out into the center of the table without asking anyone for permission. And he often did. I always believed that C.K., who had become president less than a year before the purchase of the *ADN,* saw our adventure in some ways as his own. As a writer in the *Washington Journalism Review* wrote in September 1983, "Perhaps, as the company's newly named chief executive officer, [C.K.] felt the urge to break new ground, push for his own new frontier. Overruling wary advisers and anxious board members back in Sacramento, he broke with 122 years of family tradition and decided to expand beyond their established turf ..."

His personal attachment was apparent during fairly frequent visits to Alaska, where he might don a disguising coat and beret to visit a notorious strip club or an ancient gray suit to meet the local burghers. ("This is my best suit," our multimillionaire owner had protested.) What he also did was commit more money to sustain and advance our efforts in the newspaper war.

Among many astonishing and unlikely results of the Alaska Newspaper War was this: time and again, we fashioned complex competitive strategies and then executed them successfully. I remember one we called "Operation Slingshot," designed to capitalize on some recent gains in readership and market share by redoubling effort in several key areas. It would add millions of dollars to the expenses of a newspaper that wasn't yet making any money, but it was a smart and opportunistic move for the future. C.K. signed off, we executed, and it worked.

These crucial strategic sessions were led by a charismatic, sophisticated, arrogant Harvard Business School professor named Stephen Star. He'd started working with McClatchy through a connection at the *Toronto Star*, and I know he never remotely imagined himself being in the trenches of a newspaper war in a faraway, rough-edged arena like Anchorage.

Star's central message concerned the practice of "strategic thinking" rather than "strategic planning." The difference was more than semantic. We didn't adopt discrete "strategic plans" in isolation; instead we trained ourselves to ask strategic questions about every decision with the intention of always moving toward larger goals rather than responding to short-term developments.

A good example was our decision in February 1981 to open a new front in the war by launching *ADN's* first Sunday edition since 1974, when the Joint Operating Agreement required the *Daily News* to surrender to the *Times* what was then the state's only Sunday paper.

We knew we needed to do this. Sunday newspapers were by far the most profitable advertising vehicles and we couldn't leave that spot uncontested. We also knew we'd never be a complete alternative to the *Times* until we could offer readers seven-day subscriptions. Our circulation success thus far had been built in large part by persuading *Times* subscribers to take the *News* in addition, but ultimate victory meant replacing the *Times* entirely.

Balanced against that was the knowledge that winning on the seventh day would be an especially long, expensive uphill fight. The Sunday *Times* had more subscribers and more pages than any other paper in Alaska and was still the only Sunday published in the state; matching the opposition head to head would be as risky as it would be expensive.

We settled on an unpredictable flanking maneuver instead.

While operating without a Sunday paper, we'd worked to turn our Saturday into a "weekend package," complete with color comics, a Sunday supplement magazine, a guide listing the week's TV schedule and so forth. It wasn't a fully mature Sunday paper, but it was substantial and it had fans.

We decided to keep our big package where it was on Saturday mornings for the time being and created a very different *News Sunday* paper to occupy the seventh day. Where the *Times* offered a fat paper on Sunday, ours was slim; our big paper came on Saturday, we told readers, so they had all weekend to enjoy it. *News Sunday,* in contrast, was all about breaking news and especially sports. It had a clean, modernist design and a distinctive masthead; the front page featured both news and sports in tightly edited digests. For the first few months I edited the page one news digest myself to help set a standard for what we wanted: not just copying the first paragraph of a wire-service article, but distilling the whole story, written with some flair.

News Sunday landed with a considerable splash. It didn't replace the big Sunday paper in everyone's reading habit, but it did fill a gaping void in our lineup and instantly help make the point that *ADN* was something new and modern, not just a different *Times.*

When our overall circulation strength had grown enough to buttress our confidence, we finally did migrate most extra content to Sunday and produce a more traditional package, complete with our own staff magazine. That worked, too, and soon enough our circulation lead on Sunday was greater than weekdays.

I still miss *News Sunday,* whose unique design and structure made it genuinely special. And delivering a larger paper on Saturday, giving readers all weekend to use it, still makes a lot of sense to me.

I also miss Stephen Star, who died before our battle was over but not, thankfully, until he'd seen us surge into the lead.

I recall that before Star's first visit he'd stopped at an outfitter in Seattle and equipped himself for a winter mission in Siberia. I'm sure he billed it all to McClatchy, too. But whatever his polar outfit cost and however much he charged us for his advice, Star's participation paid back multiples in dividends. Most of the ideas flowed from Anchorage or Sacramento, but they all were refined by Star.

C.K. was always part of these sessions, as was majordomo Erwin Potts, who later would become the first non-family CEO at McClatchy. A corporate news executive also attended: Frank McCulloch during the most important early meetings and Gregory Favre after Frank's departure.

Both McCulloch and Potts had served as Marines, and I'd always been infatuated with military strategies, so perhaps it was inevitable that many of our business plans would take on a martial atmosphere. I was the one assigned to pull these strategic sessions into written plans, and reviewing them now shows just as much I relied on military metaphors.

Most of our sessions would result in plans for new editorial initiatives: new sections, expanded regional coverage, more color photography. I learned to come to every session with an array of suggestions already priced out so I was ready to leap into the discussion at opportune moments with, "It would only take three people and five pages a week to do that ..."

And so we spent McClatchy's money again and again, raising the stakes and keeping pressure on our opponents. Although our efforts worked in gaining circulation and advertising, both came at a high cost, and profitability remained somewhere out on the horizon. It would have been easy, perhaps even prudent, for McClatchy to flinch or at least pull back. It never did.

Everyone was caught up in the war-room atmosphere. One of Star's lasting contributions was his description of the can-do spirit and optimism we brought to those planning sessions as "Arctic euphoria," a description I employed usefully ever after.

Chapter Sixteen
America's best newsroom

Aspirational is the adjective that best defined our attitude and goals throughout the twenty-year Alaska Newspaper War. This described us at our best and at our worst. It was the background music against which all the scenes played out, the motivation for our great successes and, on occasion, the impetus for over-reaching and some failures.

We aspired to fame and glory, and to victory. But most of all, we aspired to greatness.

This wasn't casual or incidental. We spoke about it openly, without the embarrassment we must have been too callow to feel. We challenged one another with it, threw it up as argument in budget debates, and held ourselves accountable when we failed it.

There were no grizzled newsroom veterans around to laugh good-naturedly and tell us we were silly pups. The tall mountains and distant emperor were barriers against the well-intentioned advice that otherwise might have sought to rein us in. I was thirty-five, one of the oldest people in the newsroom, when we won our second Pulitzer. We didn't know you weren't supposed to excel at small newspapers in the middle of nowhere, and so we simply kept trying.

Dougherty and I were particularly well aligned about this. We occupied innumerable long nights with visions of success and glory, and we knew the kind reputation and legacy we sought: the *Herald Tribune* of Breslin, Wolfe and Bellows; the *Washington Post* of Bradlee, Woodward and Bernstein; the *Philadelphia Inquirer* in the Gene Roberts era. We wanted people to look back fondly and say, "Yes, I was in Anchorage in those days."

Asked what we were after, I routinely replied that we wanted to create a staff that would bristle if somebody described us as "the best newspaper in America for its size."

For its size? Screw size. We wanted to be the best.

Luckily, there were a lot of talented people just as crazy as Dougherty and I.

Human beings naturally want to be part of something bigger than themselves: a church, a political party, a civic club. I discovered early on that simply telling people that they were—that this was a mission, not just a job — was often enough to make them believe it and stay.

At some point in the middle of our struggles, a group of young business students from the University of Alaska came by to interview me. "What theory of management do you use at the *Daily News*?" they asked.

Management theory? I'd never studied business, never bought a self-help book nor attended a single business seminar or workshop. I didn't know the buzz words or jargon. I thought quickly and replied that we practiced "the Hemingway Theory of Management."

Blank looks all around.

So I explained. "Ernest Hemingway once said, 'The way to find out whether or not someone is trustworthy is to trust them.' What I've discovered by doing that is that almost everybody wants to be trusted, and most of them will do anything it takes to live up to your expectations."

And that was true. We gave staffers lots of autonomy and challenged them with assignments that were way above their heads. (I once hired a young motorcycle mechanic just out of jail and on probation who went on to cover Asia as the correspondent for an international newspaper.) I'd say about eighty-five percent of the staffers we trusted did splendidly; they would have killed themselves to live up to our faith in them.

Some, of course, couldn't. But the good news about trusting people early with real responsibility was that we learned that quickly. For most of them—another ten percent of the total, say—identifying weakness meant we could provide training, adjust assignments, or otherwise find ways to put their energy and talent productively to work.

Yet no matter how careful we hired or how well we trained, about five percent, in my experience, just couldn't cut it. Once again, that became quickly apparent under our system. At that point you had to be tough enough to face facts. "This isn't going to work out," we'd tell them, and send them on their way. One reporter we let go—whom I then and now consider a friend—went on to great success elsewhere, starting a business and writing a book. The acknowledgments included something like "thanks to Howard Weaver, who gave me the time to pursue new projects." (Pro tip: firing people doesn't often work out like that, though.)

Later I would learn that even the best American newsrooms were often home to many staffers whose potential nobody knew: they never had been trusted enough to test. As a result, the fifteen percent we discovered who either needed to change or leave were left in place instead, sitting quietly on the sidelines with their heads down, hoping not to be noticed.

Given our small staff and outsized ambitions, we didn't have room for deadwood. Our answer, largely the responsibility of Dougherty as managing editor, was to give people honest job reviews and a chance to improve—and, if they didn't, a chance to work somewhere else. I'm certain our unwillingness to settle for second-rate work was key to our success.

Of course this wasn't a perfect system, and it certainly wasn't entirely the result of determined leadership, either. An essential part of our foundation was a "virtuous circle" that soon took effect in which the staff itself became its own toughest critic and a primary engine of performance.

David Halberstam described precisely this process as the foundation for Yankee greatness in his baseball book, *Summer of '49*:

> The Yankees had a tradition of playing in big games and winning. Mental toughness was enforced by the team leaders, and a succession of leadership had been established from generation to generation ... They pushed themselves and each other.
>
> It was as if everything they did advertised that this was a serious business. They were accustomed to being the best and they expected to be the best ... The Yankee players, not the managers, became the keepers of their own tradition ... If a young player came up and did not play hard, the veterans would get on him ...
>
> "It was a very tough team," [one player] later said. 'It was a team where everyone demanded complete effort. It was not a team where anyone ever said "Nice try" when you made a long run after a fly ball and didn't get it. I played on a lot of teams, and they ALL did that. But not on the Yankees. I think someone might have hit you if you said it—nice try, my ass. You weren't supposed to try; you were supposed to do it.

Having a lot of talent and ambition on a small staff at a remote newspaper created challenges of its own. We soon realized we'd inevitably lose people we didn't want to lose, usually for reasons we couldn't control: money, family situations, an ambition to work at bigger papers in bigger cities. I learned it was never advantageous to talk somebody out of leaving. But I also learned to make sure they understood where they stood and what we intended before they made a final decision. More than once a talented staffer had announced her departure without knowing she was on deck for a big promotion or change of assignment. We tried to take some of the mystery and guesswork out of the process and minimize gamesmanship simply by being more open.

Sometimes departures took us by surprise; at other times it was easy to see them coming. Perhaps the most obvious was a features editor whose wife disliked living in Alaska. I knew the editor would be leaving before long when I heard that his wife facetiously started a club called WHAT WOLF—Women Held Against Their Will On the Last Frontier. He's in Charlotte now.

We got better at retaining staff, but the longer people stayed, the fewer opportunities we could offer for promotion. There are a limited number of positions on the city desk at a small paper, for example, and an ambitious reporter who sees that assignment as the road to success is sure to become frustrated.

One answer was to try to make sure they weren't frustrated for the wrong reasons. Reporters in our newsroom could (and did) make more money than their boss. More important, we made sure everybody knew they didn't have to become an editor to influence the direction of the paper. We opened planning and decision-making to everybody, and several reporters emerged as pivotal newsroom powers over time.

At least once a year we held an all-day Saturday session to set goals and talk about ambitions. Anybody who worked in the newsroom was welcomed; nobody was required to attend. With practice I got pretty good at managing disputes, articulating consensus and making sure we ended the day with reasonably clear set of agreed expectations. Having done so, Halberstam's Yankee baseball effect took over, and we'd hold one another accountable for meeting the standards we'd set together.

Chapter Seventeen
The talent show

I know of no other small newspaper in America through this period that won more major prizes or sent more staffers per capita off to work in the big leagues than the *Anchorage Daily News*. For a variety of reasons we became a talent magnet, attracting applicants of enormous ability and potential, and that quickly becomes a feedback loop: the more good people you employ, the more other good people will want to work with you. The more prizes and success stories you accumulate, the more attractive the paper becomes to ambitious applicants.

In its prime the *News* won top national honors for features, investigative reporting, photography, sports coverage, and design. In 1994, the Society for News Design named the paper one of the twenty-five best-designed newspapers in the world; nobody could have imagined a small paper from an out-of-the-way town rising to join the ranks of London's *Daily Telegraph*, *Reforma* in Mexico City, and the *New York Times*. In 1993, the prestigious *Print* magazine devoted a nine-page, full-color spread to chronicling "A Style to Suit Alaska," which it described as "some of the most creative pages in journalism ..."

Prizes themselves are of little importance—hugely over-rated—but they established our high standards and helped build the newspaper's reputation, which in turn helped attract talent

—and that's everything. We pursued and won these honors with pragmatic intensity for just that reason.

Newspaper editors too seldom recognize that they are in a talent-driven business, no less than Hollywood or Motown. Unlike movie stars, individual staffers rarely achieved notice beyond the local scene, but their talent makes all the difference there. The difference between an adequate staffer and a gifted one, to paraphrase Mark Twain on a different subject, is "the difference between lightning and a lightning bug."

You don't need individual talent to deliver the average American newspaper—the one Molly Ivins once described as "a dry turd of lifeless facts [landing] on readers' doorsteps every morning..." But that wasn't what we intended to produce.

We wanted to showcase distinct individual voices, elegantly written prose, and pages rich with graceful notes of style. We were willing to go beyond inverted pyramids and he-said, she-said objectivity decades before that debate hit center stage in American journalism. "If it looks like a duck, if it quacks and waddles, let's just call it a duck," we reasoned; we felt no obligation to hang that attribution on some authority at the state Department of Fish and Game.

Of course we screwed up and overstepped from time to time—but not as often as you might guess, and thankfully not as often as my bosses sometimes feared.

I learned early on to ask people, "When was the last time you made a good mistake?"

A "good mistake" wasn't coming in drunk and misspelling all the names in your story. We defined it as something that was worth trying, that taught us lessons we couldn't have learned otherwise and left us equipped to do better in the future.

Most important, making good mistakes meant we were still trying new things and stretching our capabilities. The only people who don't screw up are drones who never do enough to get noticed. Creative people fail again and again; they can't survive without it.

Luckily, we enjoyed one key advantage: we were far enough away from McClatchy headquarters to get away with it.

There's no way to name or chronicle all the stars who helped raise the level of the game in Anchorage, no way even to select truly representative examples, but focusing on a few key few personalities is the only way I can think of to illustrate what a remarkable confluence of talent and dedication we enjoyed. I'll start with the indisputable first among equals.

Pat Dougherty: Over much of my career, I spent more far more waking hours with Pat than with my wife.

For more than two years at the *Alaska Advocate* we spent sixty or seventy hours working together seven days a week; through the next fifteen years we often worked almost as much at the *Daily News*. We tested one another through exhilaration and fatigue, through celebration and commiseration, in the best of times and likewise through dark days when things went terribly astray. "Trust" is far too mild a description of what I feel about him.

As a corporate executive years later, I counseled a number of newsroom leaders who were hiring managing editors and always told them, "What you need is somebody who's confident enough to come in, close the door to your office and tell you, 'Howard, you're about to screw this up in a big way.' If, after that discussion, your decision is to go ahead anyhow, she needs to be able to open the door to the newsroom and announce, 'Here's our plan...'"

Patrick was that person for me, and more: an indispensable counselor and ally whose strengths seemed always to compensate for my weaknesses and whose enthusiasm for the mission never flagged.

I've never been the most creative person in any newsroom. My strengths lay more in evaluating ideas, sprinkling "editor dust" on the good ones, and cutting the bad ones loose before they did big damage. I'm a skilled consensus-builder but at times had trouble handling conflict. My instinct and tendency is to believe colleagues can do what they say they'll do, to imagine the best potential outcome and build toward that. Not infrequently, that meant I allowed people to wander into waters too deep for their abilities.

In all these areas and more, Dougherty was an invaluable complement and counterbalance: a perpetual fount of ideas, a tough-minded manager who held people accountable, a professional with exacting standards and high expectations for himself and the staff.

We became the best of friends (his near-perfect child Katie is my god daughter), but our relationship was built first on shared professional aspirations. Each of us wanted to be part of something great, to create a newsroom that people would hear about years later and say, "It would have been great to be at the *Daily News* in those days ..." We were both presumptuous enough to believe we could pull that off and, as it turns out, stubborn enough to see it through.

Tom Kizzia: Here's a guy who came of age at *ADN* and grew into the kind of journalist I always hoped to become—insightful and intuitive; fair and even-tempered; tough-minded when he needed to be, a pussycat the rest of the time. Tom is equally a pleasure to read and a pleasure to be around, as graceful a person as he is graceful writer. I was not surprised when I learned that as a younger man he'd entered dance contests for cash prizes in Homer to help pay for building materials for his cabin. And won.

Tom was my choice for a number of make-or-break assignments. When an insane killer stalked into a remote hamlet of wilderness eccentrics and killed six people—about a third of the town's year-round residents—Tom was perhaps the only journalist in the state with the right combination of resilience, sensitivity and toughness to fly in just after the killer, help survivors open up to tell their stories and then sort out the madness for our readers. In an early story he described events at "the mountain Shangri-La" as "a sudden eruption in paradise of an immense and inexplicable evil."

Tom employed a different set of talents during his footloose journey through rural Alaska for Northcountry Journal (an assignment detailed in the next chapter), traveling by bush plane and riverboat, sleeping on living-room floors and in school gymnasiums, earning the good graces of rural people who sometimes weren't inclined to trust a city fellow. He was Huckleberry Finn with a Hampshire College pedigree, a quiet but formidable intellect thankfully attracted to GoreTex and not tweed.

And not least, he's also the guy who turned me on to Elvis Costello.

Richard Mauer: Tough investigative reporters don't always apply the toughest standards to their own work; Rich Mauer always has. I've never known a more surefooted reporter or one I trusted more to get the most complicated stories exactly right.

I did just that when I asked him to do the initial exploration of issues that later became the Pulitzer Prize series "A People in Peril" and again a few years later when he tracked down problems with another staffer's investigative work that led us to a humiliating but necessary apology.

Rich also produced an endless stream of exclusive investigative pieces, often with a focus on political scandals. With Rich on staff, there was no subject I thought we had to shy away from.

He'd come to *ADN* from the *Miami News*, at the time another struggling number two daily. By upbringing a New Yorker and still a Mets fan, he became about as Alaskan as you can get, having once researched and written about whether caribou can be kosher.

Sheila Toomey: Early one fall day in the early '80s a young intern getting ready to return to college asked if she could talk with me before leaving. It turned out she was doing graduate studies in workplace dynamics, or something like that, and wanted to test some of her observations about our newsroom power structure.

The intern was bright and observant and had reached several interesting conclusions, but the most intriguing by far was her discussion of staff writer Sheila Toomey, a relatively recent addition who had come to us not from another newspaper but (shudder) broadcasting. While Sheila had no masthead title or official slot on the organization charts, the intern observed, she was nonetheless one of the most powerful people in the newsroom.

I knew Sheila was special, but I hadn't yet thought about her quite that way. The more I considered it, the more obvious the conclusion became: yes, she was a major influence in the newsroom.

Another New Yorker, Sheila had spent more time as a social worker than reporter at that point, but her instinct for news was as strong as that of a salmon headed homeward. She was endlessly fascinated by strange, compelling stories, and—unlike many report-ers—didn't clinch up when it came time to tell them, laying them out for readers just as they had captured her own capacious imagination.

"People read crime stories until they come to the part where they can think, 'Oh, that won't happen to me. I never go to that part of town, I don't sell drugs or whatever,'" she once told me. "Once I figured that out, I started putting all that stuff at the end of the story."

She brought her formidable curiosity to whatever task was at hand. Overhearing her telephone interviews—hard to avoid, given her booming voice—became a kind of newsroom hobby, providing stories we loved to trade with one another.

"You should have heard Sheila on that last call: 'How big was the pool of blood?' ... 'Does your mother know you've been doing this?'" I once considered making a recording of her on the telephone that could be played in tight-assed newsrooms that needed a little life.

Kathleen McCoy: Typically enough, plenty of the folks in our newsroom had a propensity to tilt decidedly toward "hard news," often disdaining features, slice of life, and profile stories. Fortunately, we found a features champion with the spunk and talent to show them why that was wrong.

Kathleen could occupy that ground partly because she'd already proved herself on more traditional, tough-guy assignments. She'd worked at small newspapers in California and then the venerable *Nome Nugget*, about a hundred miles south of the Arctic Circle and 160 miles east of Russia. Her bravura performance walking up an icy beach at the end of the 1,000-mile long Iditarod sled dog race after her snowmachine ran out of gas (the driver apparently spent her money on drugs) made believers throughout the newsroom.

She also had the chops to demonstrate what she wanted from her staffers, herself a graceful writer with an uncommon eye for human details. Along with a handful of other top staffers, she'd pulled a laboring oar on the Pulitzer-winning "People in Peril" series, chronicling especially sensitive stories about struggles for sobriety in one small Indian town.

Kathleen and a cadre of talented feature writers—Debra McKinney, George Bryson, Doug O'Hara, and others—more than held their own in the newsroom and gave our coverage an extra dimension.

Richard Murphy: It's tempting to say Murphy had one of the easiest editing assignments at the paper—being photo editor in a place as photogenic as Alaska. He had also inherited a tradition of excellence and a pretty fair staff from his predecessors in the job.

Yet it's what Murphy did with that legacy that marked him as special. He turned his staff into an enthusiastic and opportunistic tribe unwilling to accept second-best. They started out good and kept getting better throughout his tenure, a culture of continuous improvement. Somebody once said of Alabama football legend Bear Bryant that "he could take his team and beat yours, or take yours and beat his." That describes Murphy coaching his staff to the top ranks of American photojournalism. In 1990 they finished as one of three finalists in the Pulitzer competition, turning in a remarkable portfolio I still think deserved to win for *Exxon Valdez* coverage.

I also think of Murphy whenever I remember the disgruntled reader who called and asked to speak to "an editor" about the paper's "persistent anti-Irish bias."

I wanted to ask which editor he'd prefer: the city editor, Mike Doogan; the editorial page editor, Mike Carey; Kathleen McCoy, the features editor; or maybe the photo editor, Richard Murphy? Failing with them, I could have connected him with the managing editor, a guy named Patrick Dougherty. As I recall, that caller, unlike many, ultimately hung up happy.

Chapter Eighteen
Alaska's tribal fire

Good plans, McClatchy money, and a talented staff could not themselves the battle win. We had to execute across a broad range of initiatives under constant pressure to excel. God bless that staff; they did it again and again.

The aspirations that motivated our newsroom team from my earliest days as editor never were eclipsed; instead they grew and matured as the war raged on. By 1987, we had the *Anchorage Times* fixed squarely in our sights, and we knew it. The enemy might not believe our circulation numbers, but we did, and we knew those readers were our newsroom's only reliable friends.

Sooner or later a good newsroom is bound to piss off politicians and advertisers, and sooner or later even the best publisher worries about that. The allies we knew we could always count on were satisfied readers who kept paying us for what we did.

As long as circulation grew and we were gaining on the *Times*, there would be money to keep up the fight. We hung a banner above the coffee machine in the newsroom that said "We Work for the Readers"—and we meant it.

Dougherty in particular was always ready to toss out journalistic convention if it ran contrary to that purpose. For example, as local news editor in the early days of the war, he determined that when politicians answered campaign questionnaires with political doublespeak, we wouldn't run it. He'd offer them a second chance to be specific, but then printed "the candidate was not responsive to this question" in place of their non-response.

Was that fair, I wondered? "Howard, they didn't answer," Patrick insisted. "Just putting some words in the blank isn't the same as answering. Would you make us print it untranslated if they answered in French?"

He was right; readers were better served if we exercised judgment and common sense on their behalf, and so we did.

I drew the line, however, at one further suggestion: Whenever candidates listed "the Bible" as their favorite book, Dougherty (a Baylor grad from the era of mandatory chapel) wanted to make them prove it by administering a pop quiz to make sure they really knew crap from Corinthians. I wouldn't go there, though I see now that I probably should have.

We got a good bit of favorable notice in the trade press for unorthodox campaigns and atypical behavior. Dougherty professed amazement. "Damn, you know? The cutting edge of American journalism can't be more than a half-inch out there ..."

We likewise waged a sustained, sometimes successful campaign against those boring-but-traditional stories some called MEGOs—My Eyes Glaze Over.

Many days there would be uneventful, predictable stories in the *Times* and on all the local TV newscasts that we'd ignored entirely. A politician's press conference didn't get automatic coverage in the *Daily News*; he had to say something newsworthy. An incremental, predictable development in a continuing story might not make the paper, either.

Naturally these decisions didn't sit well with politicians and publicists who were used to having press coverage on their terms and about their agenda. Sooner or later I'd get a call from the publisher asking, "Everybody else in town had this story. Why didn't we?"

If I didn't know the answer offhand (and I wasn't much of a micromanager) I'd walk dutifully out to the city desk to find out.

I learned over time not to ask "Why didn't we cover this?" but "What were you doing instead?" Lethargy or ignorance weren't good excuses, but anything focused on trying to get better stories into the paper was, and I supported them.

I can't say my publishers always agreed, but they came to expect to hear it. And after all, readership was still going up.

The editor of *The Economist*—naturally an Englishman, with the delightfully Dickensian name of Dudley Fishburn—was a friend of our owner, C.K. McClatchy, who asked me to look after Fishburn when he visited Alaska during this era. I was thrilled; as one of perhaps a handful of Alaskans with an *Economist* subscription, I was in awe of the sophistication, range and astonishingly authoritative voice of the magazine, and relished a chance to spend time with the editor.

I particularly admired its willingness to use an opinion piece or editorial— "leading article," in British terms—as the cover story. I asked him to meet with our editorial board to talk about the role of opinion journalism.

"We see our editorials as memoranda to the people who run the world, telling them what to do," he told us. My talented but rather conventional editorial page editor was quite taken aback. "But how can you be sure enough to tell everybody what to do?" she asked him. He sat up straighter and arched an eyebrow as he answered: "Madam, if you require everything to add up to one-hundred percent, you'll run a very tight-assed little newspaper, won't you?"

In truth, American newsrooms in those days tended to be astonishingly constipated places where change came grudgingly, if at all. "Like the French bureaucracy," somebody once told me. "Nothing should ever be done for the first time." This was, of course, a recipe for irrelevancy in the fast-changing society we served, and we were determined that no matter what, the *Anchorage Daily News* would not become irrelevant.

"Your relationship with readers should be like any other romance," I'd tell staffers. "Everybody wants to be loved, but there's a lot more security in being needed."

Years later I'd learn to call this the "value proposition" newspapers should offer readers: become necessary. Trust that people will come to the paper not because they liked us or felt obligated, but because we gave them things they needed.

Luckily "being needed" offers a huge portfolio of opportunities because readers need a lot more than city council stories. People also need to be entertained and amused. They need to know why the hockey team can't score on the power play, and whether the local orchestra is worth listening to. They need us, in the words of British journalist and social critic Henry Fairlie, to "see life steady and see it whole."

I'd been in love with that phrase and that concept since I first encountered it in my salad days at the *Advocate*, but resisting traditional "eat your broccoli" news judgment and concentrating on compelling stories instead remained a constant struggle. Innovation has always been an uphill battle in American newsrooms.

We wanted to write about real life and not agendas. The paper's most graceful writer, Tom Kizzia, was dispatched for a months-long meander across the vast rural reaches of the state and asked to send back stories, not articles. We published these as "Northcountry Journal."

Above all, we wanted to avoid journalism-as-usual, and I remember sending him off with a specific warning: if you put the day of the week in the lead, we'll bring you home. He recently recalled more about those instructions: "Somewhere I still have the three-by-five card you and Pat gave me as I set out on Northcountry Journal, with words of advice. I remember a few off hand. 'If you come across a good news story in a village, turn and walk in the other direction' and 'If you feel the need to use a term of anthropology, lie down and breathe deeply until the feeling passes.'"

On another occasion, Tom and John Tetpon, one of the few Alaska Natives on staff, teamed up to report on "Speak Inupiat

Day" with a story written entirely *in* Inupiat —an effort we hoped might remind Alaskans of one thing that made the state so special.

Tom later called on his deep insights into rural culture and his reporting from Northcountry Journal to produce a compelling book, *The Wake of the Unseen Object*, which offers an unmatched, clear-eyed view of daily life in rural Alaska in those crucial times.

This memo to the city desk from David Hulen, who inherited the beat Tom created in covering rural Alaska, provides a sense of how we went looking for the kinds of stories newspaper readers didn't often see:

It's 12:45 in the morning Tuesday. I got back to Nome at midnight. It was a good, long day—we left town late in the morning and ended up going about twenty miles southwest, out in the ocean and onto the ice. One twenty-foot boat—Charlie Johnson in command, his son and his thirty-something nephew with the rifles, one of the scientists from NOAA with the test kit, and your correspondent with water-proof notebook and idiot-proof camera.

At one point, deep in the endless, swirling slush (imagine driving a little boat around the top of a cocktail glass the size of Virginia, chasing after wild animals with flippers), the boys spotted a mess of bearded seals—oogruks. They shot at the biggest one. They hit. It looked to be maybe 300 yards off across the ice, which has big cracks and many puddles and ridges and little channels of water. Charlie drives the boat up on a flat pan of ice, and he and the boys WALK ACROSS THE FUCKING ICE for the seal. They drag it a bit and decide it's too heavy. They ask how I feel about walking out to the seal. They're going to just butcher it out there.

Truth is, I feel terrified. But, always the gracious guest, I help them plant the anchor in the ice and we all ended up

WALKING ACROSS THE FUCKING ICE to get to the seal, stepping over these fucking crevasses where you look down and see about three or four layers of icebergs through blue water God-knows-how-deep. The most prevalent sound was the drip-drip-drip of the ice melting. Every once in a while you'd hear a huge crash—an iceberg collapsing.

The seal was 7 1/2 feet long. It was a pretty primal scene— the three hunters pulling it across the ice with a rope, like generations of Inupiat before them. And of course they lugged this orange cooler filled with testing equipment so they could put on their rubber gloves and take tissue samples. And when we got back to the boat, we all swigged out of the big bottle of Classic Coke.

Weather got kind of wild coming back—once we were out of the ice it was really windy and choppy—but by the time we reached Nome, the wind had died and there was a massive pink moon rising. What a weird place Nome is, more depressing, to me, than Bethel, but there are some pretty interesting characters.

I'll check in later today; seeing how I'm here and everything, I'm not in any big rush to get back. Right now I'm figuring Wednesday or Thursday.

And remember: the worst day oogruk hunting beats the best day working. Or something like that.

With experience, our planning sessions and countless newsroom discussions distilled into a coherent philosophy of coverage based on fearlessness, storytelling, and a sense of community. Perhaps the best way to describe it is by telling you about the Order of the Tribal Fire.

In the early 1980s I'd been invited to the inaugural session of New Directions for News, one of the earliest think-tank efforts aimed at imagining different futures for the news business. I was in my early thirties, not yet jaded to the shadow theater of such conferences, and the location (the Rand Corporation in Santa Monica) and the presence of professional "innovation facilitators" (who knew?) impressed me mightily.

Yet the image that stuck with me most firmly had come up almost incidentally; I'll be surprised if anybody else remembers it at all. During one discussion, an editor from Los Angeles—I'm sorry to have forgotten her name—talked about newspapers' role in defining communities. Her metaphor was of the newspaper serving as "the tribal fire," something like the place where bands of ancient peoples must have gathered to exchange the stories that would define them as a culture. I especially liked with the way she dismissed television's potential in that role, and I can recall it still: "the flickering box yields an unsteady light, and strangely little warmth.")

I remembered her metaphor as we worked to define the role we sought for the *Daily News*, and it fitted our intentions perfectly. We wanted to be Alaska's tribal fire—the place where Alaskans gathered to tell the stories that defined us as a people. I employed the analogy constantly, at one point instituting the "Order of the Tribal Fire" award I'd give to staffers whose work best reflected our ambitions.

Many years later an anonymous blogger who set out to ridicule and chastise the *Daily News* used "Tribal Fires" as the name for his site, which struck me then as mean-spirited theft. Later it occurred to me that I'd appropriated the idea myself from the conference. (Still, he also used the *nom de plume* of "Billy Muldoon," taken from a character I'd invented for my metro column years before. The mature reaction is to remember that imitation is flattery, I suppose. I'll keep trying.)

Alaskans needed—and still need—such a sense of shared community. With the exception of Indians, Eskimos, and Aleuts, Alaskans mostly live in towns like Anchorage or along the few highways that connect them, yet they identify with wilderness and think of themselves as pioneers. We aimed to scratch that itch. We named our Sunday magazine *We Alaskans,* an overt effort aimed at celebrating and defining our unique society. The magazine ran long narrative stories that gave breathing room to a cadre of writers who belong with the best ever published in a newspaper. In its pages and throughout the paper we featured stories about sled dog races and mountain climbers and features like "Alaska's Toughest Woman."

We honed our own sense of mission purposefully, working to create a culture where everybody had a voice in setting priorities and defining our objectives.

I'd learned a little about "organizational development" from my wife, who was busily helping define and shape social service non-profits in Alaska, and I employed those techniques to run planning sessions where we collaborated in defining our intentions. Editorial cartoonist Peter Dunlap-Shohl, then a youngster in his twenties, remembered one session:

> I remember a Saturday staff meeting that was a key moment for me in crystallizing my idea of the Daily News. To start with, the very idea that management would invite rank and file (some of us more rank than others) to come and kick around the big picture of what we were supposed to be doing is novel enough that it bears mention. The fact that so many of us, from inputter to investigative reporter, showed up on a day off to be paid only in bagels tells you something about how devoted we were to the *ADN.*
>
> What exactly were we trying to accomplish in the newsroom? That's what we were there to clarify. [Howard] started us off by writing a proposed set of our top three goals. That was many years ago and I'm fuzzy on many details. The first was probably something like "To speak truth to power," the second was maybe along the lines of "To tell Alaska's stories." The third, however, I remember clearly. It was: "And to have fun."

I remember this one for two reasons. First, I agreed completely. If you are going to devote yourself to something for a minimum of eight hours a day, it better be fun ... I also believe that if the staff isn't having fun, you can forget about the reader enjoying what they write or photograph or draw.

The second reason this sticks in my mind was the horrified reaction it got. Having fun was seen as too frivolous by some of the attendees [who] argued, if I remember right, that the final goal should be "To serve the community." The sense that we were on a mission was a major mark of our paper.

I saw no need to choose one at the expense of the other, though. So while we had our share of fun along the way, we likewise focused our growing staff and increasing capabilities on watchdog journalism, always a priority but not always a possibility for the paper in its pauper days. The troubled single term of one Alaska governor in this period—Bill Sheffield—is illustrative.

Throughout his term from 1982 to 1986, Sheffield was often the target of negative stories and press criticism and ultimately faced both indictment and impeachment, though neither came to pass. Like countless politicians before and since, he thought the press was prejudiced against him.

It's not surprising he was caught unaware. In "Lessons of the Sheffield Years," a speech to the Fairbanks Press Club in 1991, I talked about the role Alaska's changing press corps played in his troubles:

The years of William Jennings Sheffield were not a happy time for government in Alaska. Caught in a rising tide of change—changing economics, yes, but more importantly of changing expectations—the governor proved inadequate to the tasks at hand. [His] tenure ended in rejection and defeat.

It does not surprise us to learn that he does not think that was his fault. Instead, he blames the press. Probably you will find it equally unsurprising that I do not agree. Our 'blame' attaches only thus: we caught him often enough in his inadequacies and told those stories plainly enough that they could not be hidden even by the most ambitious public relations campaign in Alaska's political history ...

A governor in an earlier Alaska might never have faced the circumstances that led Bill Sheffield to stumble. If he had been, he probably wouldn't have been caught. And if he was, people very well might not have minded...

[But] the press changed ... Just as the challenge of governing [Alaska] was growing in complexity, reporters across the state reached levels of sophistication that allowed detailed examination. We became more aggressive—and better able to perform.

Criticism and scandal stuck to the man we called the Velcro Governor. Just after his election he started soliciting donations to repay $600,000 in personal funds he'd loaned to the campaign—definitely unseemly and perhaps illegal. Later he spent public money to campaign across the state at elaborate "town hall meetings" that really were PR events. He steered a $9 million contract to a Fairbanks labor leader who had helped bankroll his campaign.

That transaction caught the attention of a prosecutor and grand jury in Juneau, a fact that became public when enterprising *Daily News* reporter John Lindback found copies of documents from the grand jury session in a capitol waste can. Commenting on page after page of testimony marked by the governor's "failed memory," the grand jury decided not to indict him but instead declared him unfit for public service and recommended impeachment.

When the state senate convened in July 1985 for impeachment hearings, I went to Juneau with five reporters and an editor, an unmatched commitment in the history of Alaska journalism. The blanket coverage dominated our front pages every day for two weeks: stories, of course, and also a boxed summary of events, a preview of the coming day's action, and highlighted quotes from the preceding day. I reported extensively and wrote commentary and analysis every day.

When it was over and the senate failed to impeach on a 12-8 vote, I used my column to put the experience in perspective for Alaska:

> Chicago columnist Mike Royko made fun of us for getting all excited about alleged behavior that wouldn't have even tripped the scandal meter in his town. A Louisiana newspaper said that even if Bill Sheffield was guilty of everything he was charged with, he could still come down there and run as a reform candidate.
>
> Basically, they snickered. I guess they think we're naive.
>
> I'm glad. If Alaskans can still get mad about things that wouldn't even make the paper in Chicago, there's hope for us still.
>
> Once more, with feeling: We don't give a damn how they do it Outside.

A year later, in April 1986, the paper took on another branch of government, bringing a lawsuit against the Alaska Legislature itself to stop implementation of the state budget because it had been constructed by what we called "a shadow legislature" at illegal secret meetings. Backed by our longtime lawyer John McKay, we did what we usually did with his representation: we won. The Superior Court in Juneau ruled in our favor on all the merits and issued an injunction to force legislators back into the open. By the time the Alaska Supreme Court ruled the issue "non-justiciable" and thus beyond the reach of lawsuit, our point had been made.

Legislative leaders were furious at us. Readers? Not so much.

About this time we adopted another newsroom motto, one I cribbed from the Hell's Angels motorcycle club and had emblazoned on bright red enamel pins I distributed to the staff. The Angels' motto was "Ride Hard, Die Free." For us it became "Write Hard, Die Free." Critics sometimes described this as radical and extreme. We just wrote harder and wore the pins and jacket patches with pride for years thereafter.

Along the way we naturally managed to make large groups of readers angry for one reason or another. Our quest for independent judgment and tough-mindedness sometimes blinded us to how stories would affect individual readers, and we went too far. I remember a front-page apology I thought was called for after we ran a murder story with unnecessarily graphic details including police speculation that the killer had licked the victim's blood from the knife he used.

During the first Gulf War, we managed to alienate a far larger percentage of readers for running an important story that was entirely accurate—and, I came to understand, was presented with far too little regard for its effect on readers.

In the middle Operation Desert Storm in February 1991 we undertook to answer a question that had been raised widely in Alaska and elsewhere: was the trans-Alaska pipeline a likely target for terrorist sabotage, and if so, was it vulnerable?

We *knew* it was vulnerable. Hell, we'd proved it years before with the *Alaska Advocate*'s smoke grenade.

This time we took a more sophisticated look. Kim Farraro, the top-notch reporter we assigned, was a national award-winner who later would go to work for the *New York Times*. She explored the issues extensively. For one thing, we were able to report that the experts we consulted said it probably wasn't a likely target; the short-term damage done by interrupting the flow of oil wouldn't be all that significant in a global context.

We also anticipated objections to our story—although, as it turned out, not nearly enough. We ran a small editor's note with the page-one story that directly addressed whether our story discussing the possibility of attack made one more likely. "The experts we talked with—and common sense—say no," I said. "Terrorists actually attempting to target the pipeline surely would know more than a newspaper article will discuss ..."

That disclaimer was hugely overshadowed by the story itself, complete with a multi-column, full-color infographic and map that identified with photos twelve areas that experts judged most at risk. It ran under a bold headline: "Trans-Alaska Pipeline: Areas vulnerable to terrorist attack."

"Why don't you just send your goddamned map to Saddam Hussein, you traitor?" one of hundreds of furious callers yelled into my telephone early that February morning.

"My husband works on the pipeline and here you are showing people how to kill him," said another outraged caller.

Official reaction was no more restrained. Alaska's U.S. senators condemned our report, as did the global president of British Petroleum. BP and all the other oil companies operating in Alaska launched an immediate advertising boycott.

Along with a number of other editors, I manfully answered the phone for several hours. After a dozen calls I realized there was no way I could convince them of our logic: for instance, that there were far more detailed maps and engineering diagrams of the pipeline in widely available federal environmental impact statements on file at many public libraries any terrorist could access.

By the end of the day I was physically and emotionally exhausted. Was this it, I wondered, the One Big Mistake I'd secretly feared would one day undermine all the progress and success we'd worked so hard to achieve? By the end of the day I wanted nothing more than to get into bed and pull the covers over my head. Instead I went to a hockey game, as planned. Never let 'em see you sweat.

By great good fortune I was leaving the next day for vacation in Hawaii, visiting the guy Hawaiians would call my "hanai dad," mentor and guru Paul Goodrich.

A World War II Marine hero, former city cop, and once director of the state Department of Revenue in Anchorage, Paul was always a steadying influence and a source of invaluable perspective. After my own dad's early death I'd often turned to Paul, a good friend's father, for advice and guidance.

An objective observer probably would say I whined and maybe even whimpered as we sat on Paul's lanai in Kealakekua and talked late into the night about my latest shitstorm. When I finished, his take on the situation was, as always, impeccable: "Well, you haven't told me anything that's going to kill you, or cost you your job, or even make your dingus fall off," he said.

I checked, and he was right. I didn't feel great right away, but I felt better.

We also learned to deal with irate readers fairly regularly when they became angry with columnist Mike Doogan, another weapon in the arsenal we assembled for our war against the *Times* and boring newspapers in general. Mike was rarely boring.

Doogan—at this writing a state legislator, and a good one—is among the rarest of Alaskans: a white guy whose roots in the country run back three generations. The progeny of gold-rush boomers and pioneers in Interior Alaska, he was a Fairbanks guy who'd moved to Anchorage and started his newspapering at the *Anchorage Times*.

Smug as we were, we naturally counted that as a strike or two against him, but he was too good a newsman to last long at the *Times* and too good for us to ignore. He'd been Sunday editor there, one of the most important jobs in the newsroom, but he just wasn't cut out to work under the paper's establishment bias and quixotic decision-making. He moved to the city desk at *ADN* and quickly began making a difference.

He recalls getting his columnist job this way in the preface to one of the books he's written since:

> Early in 1990 I was working as an assistant city editor
> for the Anchorage Daily News when the newspaper

went in short order from having two local columnists to having none.

The people who ran the newspaper needed to fill that hole PDQ. My entire job interview went like this.

Howard Weaver, the newspaper's top editor at the time, called me into his office and said, 'Would you like to be our Metro columnist?'

"Yes," I said.

"You are," he said.

I hope I was that clever. I'm sure Mike was, and he would be for years afterward, certainly the best and highest profile Alaska columnist of our generation, for my money the best ever. He handled language like any good Irishman, treating it right and using it hard. He turned phrases and created images better than anybody. I remember a comment in a column about a criminal waiting to be sentenced for some particularly heinous crime. "I hope he spends at least the next twenty years married to the guy with the most cigarettes," Mike wrote.

I had raised the idea of moving Doogan into the columnist slot months earlier as a way to make our paper different than the *Times* and to capture attention. I cautioned in making the pitch in a strategic-plan memo that "high profile doesn't come cheaply, and Mike isn't muzzle-able."

As I'd anticipated, he was a big talent and often enough a big pain in the ass. He always shouldered more than his share of the irate reader calls (although I also got a few) and I managed to deflect most of the grief aimed his way by the publisher or others. On the very rare occasion when I had to play a trump card, he could shut up and soldier on, but in general we both knew his column was going to be honest or worthless. Mike and I both wanted honest.

People often asked me how the *Daily News* could win in Anchorage when its coverage was so aggressive and its editorial policy generally more liberal than the *Times* or prevailing community attitudes. My short answer: Americans don't mind if you have an opinion as long as you're also willing to listen to theirs.

And we listened. We were "interactive" decades before interactive became cool.

Starting in the 1980s, we got regular feedback from a large community advisory board specifically selected to represent a diversity of interests, especially interests different than our own. We gave regular op-ed columns to readers on rotating six-month assignments, again selecting the widest range of views. We published page after page of letters to the editor, more than most newspapers ten times our size, and every year we threw an open house to celebrate these contributions.

Within the paper we referred to that event fondly as "The Letter Writers' Ball," and over time it became a remarkable celebration of free speech, one of my favorite events of the year. The publisher was skeptical of the idea at first, fearful that a collection of letter-writers might grow volatile; he hired off-duty cops for security.

"No need to worry," I promised. "These are people who like to talk and argue and let off steam. The guy you need to worry about is alone in an upstairs room somewhere right now cleaning his moose rifle." As Editorial Page Editor Mike Carey often observed about the letter-writers, "Postage stamps are cheaper than therapy."

Every week we sent accuracy questionnaires to people mentioned in news stories to ask whether we'd gotten the story right. I asked an administrative assistant to pick recipients without supervision to guard against selection bias. We gave cash bonuses to editors encouraging them to become familiar with community institutions— by arranging a tour of the Air Force base, perhaps, or studying religious congregations in town. We said yes to every request for public speakers.

It worked. Both anecdotally and in numerous professional readership surveys, we scored high on community awareness. Readers picked us as most likely "to watch out for the interests of people like me" and gave us high marks for fairness—sometimes noting that we were equally tough on all sides.

Meanwhile the *Times* was running the same operation it always had: distant, arrogant, aloof. It wouldn't run letters critical of the paper. There was an enemies list of people whose names couldn't appear in the paper. Declarations from their favorites were reported uncritically while opponents faced blistering questioning and characterizations—when the *Times* mentioned them at all.

People regularly expressed amazement that the *Daily News* was winning the war for readers. For reasons like these, it didn't surprise me at all.

Chapter Nineteen
Looking around the corners

Although I didn't think of it this way at the time, I had spent the years between 1972 and 1992 assembling a playbook for practicing a distinctive style of journalism: reader-centered, philosophically transparent, and intellectually aggressive. The lessons we accumulated not only helped us defeat the *Anchorage Times* but would remain relevant long beyond its demise.

Over the years, we anticipated in surprising ways the media transformations that were to upend traditional newspaper journalism in the decades to come. We got a lot of things right—sometimes by trial and error, itself a novelty for most newspapers—and we saw beyond the horizon farther than you'd imagine.

Some of that we demonstrated by behavior: our retreat from the tired standards of objectivity; a constant search for voice, whether in describing life in rural villages for urban readers or in spelling out plainly how lawmakers caved in to oil interests; and extensive outreach to readers through guest columns, advisory boards, accuracy surveys, community meetings and the like.

As we progressed we abandoned—sometimes emphatically, sometimes covertly—the dominant paradigm of he-said-she-said "objectivity," realizing without knowing the words for it that what NYU Professor Jay Rosen would later name the "View From Nowhere" served neither readers nor reporters best. I told staffers, students and civic club audiences a hundred times that I had come to understand that "truth is a plural noun," that the notion of "getting both sides" of a story was a fiction that hardly ever fit the real world.

Throughout the war we turned our back on reporting "news of record" and looked instead for news of relevance. We let our opponents at the *Times* and television stations spend their limited energies on agenda-driven coverage of city council meetings; forced to choose, we preferred to root out corrupt city managers instead. We took the legendary *Philadelphia Inquirer* Gene Roberts at his word when we read his observation that, "Not all news breaks. There is also news that trickles, and seeps, and oozes."

I preached the need to remember we did journalism *for* readers, not *to* them. I renounced the Divine Right of Journalists as justification for anything we did. In a fight to the death where circulation was the only meaningful scorecard, we came to understand with practical certainty the necessity of a new relationship with readers, dramatically modifying the top-down Editor As God structure built into the very fabric of American newspapers.

Against my expectations I faced unending push-back not only from professional peers in the company and industry but likewise many of the staffers we were trying to empower. Agreeing that it was time to institute yet another change from the status quo, Dougherty once sighed, "Okay, I'll go try to sell this to the Superior Court judges on the copy desk."

As a result of such experiences, it came as no surprise to me, many years later, to see how reluctantly newsrooms adapted to the changing realities of a newly digital world.

We kept trying. We abandoned traditional newspaper design for a radical new look, especially in "Impulse," a new section aimed at young readers, finally winning a disagreement with traditionalist skeptics in Sacramento by arguing the pages should be compared not with other newspapers but rather MTV and CD covers, their natural peers. The CEO relented with this caution: "Just be sure you use type the way God intended." I choked back the impulse to ask whether he'd found those instructions in Deuteronomy or Leviticus.

We worked to live up to the promise I made years before in an early *Advocate* column, to "resemble, on balance, more the guerrilla soldier than the regimented Redcoat...[seeing ourselves] not as part of the organized system but as an alternative to it... [as] civilization's cheerleader and society's scold."

Much of what made our operation different was the product of competitive imperatives and just such hard-won experience. Some of it, though, was the result of foresight. That was especially apparent in our early recognition of the digital tsunami even then building offshore.

Our first digital success came in harnessing an early Macintosh computer to a database program to examine campaign contributions. In July, 1986, *Time* magazine took note of our pioneering in an article headlined "New Paths to Buried Treasure: Computers are revolutionizing investigative journalism." It featured a photo of reporter Rich Mauer and contributor Larry Makinson and described how their 1985 database project uncovered "a nest of questionable schemes," including one that bundled twenty seemingly independent contributions to one state senator on one day. "Without the computer, this information would have remained buried like a treasure chest at the bottom of the sea," Makinson told them.

That success was another victory for a newsroom management system that rewarded initiative and had little fear of failure. Nobody commissioned Mauer or Makinson to pioneer computer-assisted reporting. The Macintosh they used had very little file storage, but a breakthrough came when Makinson discovered Iomega's Bernoulli Box, a Mac-compatible peripheral that could hold a phenomenal five megabytes of data on removable cartridges. I give Publisher Grilly credit for approving the $2,000 purchase, though for a long time thereafter the term "Bernoulli Box" was applied to any questionable newsroom purchase request.

In 1987 I was invited to speak at a gathering of the somewhat grandly imagined Alaska Future Society, and of course I chose to talk about the future of news and information. By then I was online myself, on local electronic bulletin boards (BBS systems) and global services like CompuServe and Dialog, and I'd already formed strong ideas about how things were going to change.

I began the speech by recounting how many newspaper editors a generation earlier had seen television only as a competitor, never responding to the ways it had changed storytelling. Citing "competition," some wouldn't even publish TV schedules. Here was my interpretation:

> [T]he editors who recognized that television was a force to be reckoned with were able to adapt, to strengthen their report as a result. Today they publish successful, useful newspapers. The other guys are gone.
>
> A very strong parallel can be drawn between that experience and the newspaper editor of today who watches the computer revolution and tries to determine what that will mean for the newspaper of tomorrow.
>
> Without question, computerization has changed and will continue to change the nature of successful newspapers...
>
> It's clear that I think the press in general, and newspapers in particular, play a role that we need to keep alive in our society. But I don't kid myself into believing that simply because we are important, that we are guaranteed a successful future.

Then I talked some about changes that had already come to the world in which I worked: obvious things like twenty-four-hour cable news, *USA Today*, increasing numbers of niche magazines serving special interests. I also noted some less obvious changes:

how reliable, affordable worldwide telephone service and our increasingly well-traveled audience changed expectations of what we should deliver. But I saved the most significant for last:

> For all that, it's obvious that the biggest revolutionary factor in a newspaperman's life today is the computer:
>
> Newspapers will change physically because of what computers can do for them and readers.
>
> And, more importantly by far, computers will change the nature of what readers expect and what newspapers deliver in the future.
>
> The very nature of technological change means it is difficult to predict what form it will take... But we can confidently predict what role newspapers may play in any of several scenarios:
>
> If inexpensive, widespread personal telecommunications like the French experience with Minitel becomes common, newspapers will offer increasing On-Line services to supplement the more general content of their newsprint publication ...
>
> One of the most exciting developments coming for publishing is the refinement of HYPERTEXT, an electronic publishing system that lets readers access information along many different avenues, and not just the linear fact-follows-fact method we now use.
>
> If the development of superconductors allows increasing miniaturization, as predicted, wrist-sized personal computers may link us all with databases easily and instantly from anywhere we work ... and newspapers will have to adapt to that.
>
> Obviously, I don't know precisely which of those scenarios or dozens of others will come true. But I do know that successful newspapers will adapt and adopt those

new technologies; and like the old fogies who thought television was a passing fad, the others will fade away.

More important than those exciting physical changes that technology may bring is the fact that computers and the liberation they bring will change our expectations about news and information.

As a user of computer information services myself, one thing I have experienced most strongly is the fact that access to the speed and depth of information computers bring changes our expectations forever. I am no longer satisfied with a library that closes its doors at 9 p.m., because I know I can dial up a reference service at any time of the day or night and find the information I need.

But pure volume of information is not what readers need—or even what they want. In fact, we are awash in information. We need not more information, but more useable information...

The newspaper of tomorrow must think of itself as being in the information business, not the printing business, and then it will see that the technological changes on the horizon are opportunities, and not problems.

By the next year, 1988, readers with computers and modems could access the contents of the *Anchorage Daily News* online—years before the advent of the World Wide Web or graphical browsers. Surely ours was one of the first newspapers anywhere to create an online presence.

We made that jump via a BBS running on Red Ryder software. Features Editor Gary Nielson, like me a personal computer hobbyist, worked with a local computer consultant to launch the system on a spare Macintosh computer sitting out of the way on a desk in the corner. We used a Mac database program to gather articles from our print content-management system that we then posted on the plain-text BBS we called "The Front Page." An April 1988 article in the publication *MACazine* applauded us for including a visitors' guide for tourists, letters to the editor, and an interactive feature inviting readers to help write a collaborative Alaska novel.

We also posted classified advertising from the paper, too, though nobody in the advertising department or elsewhere could see much future in that.

Our BBS project of course had no staff, no budget, and no permission to exist. It languished in the shadows for about a year and finally blinked out.

By August 1989 I had refined my ideas somewhat and begun to talk about how to apply these notions broadly to the newspaper business. In a memo to the McClatchy strategic-planning group I complained that the newspaper industry was responding to the coming changes mainly "by seeking legal and legislative restrictions" against electronic competitors. That was clearly failing even then, and I argued for direct competition—to start playing offense, if you will:

> We have advantages and strengths to play to if we choose. We have the franchise today as Anchorage's primary information source. We have an enormous information base, comprised both of the historical record of what we've covered and the material we generate and receive every day.
>
> Yet we offer that information in one way at one time of day only: a newspaper printed shortly after midnight and delivered before breakfast.
>
> Voice information systems, computer access avenues and other outreach efforts could change that. We can find ways to offer closing stocks in the afternoon, research into the 1985 legislature, more in-depth reporting on Lebanon than appeared in our pages. We can do all that with off-the-shelf, present day technology.

By doing so, we also preempt others from making a move into those areas and position ourselves to do even more—computerized classifieds, talking Yellow Pages, etc.—in the future.

It can be expensive, and we need to find out if we can make it pay.

The strategic question: What are we waiting for?

In April 1990 I expanded my emerging theory of changing information climates in a speech to the Alaska Library Society that I called "The End of Smart on the Top, Dumb on the Bottom." Now I was thinking about something more radical than supplementing printed newspapers with electronic online services. I was pondering what I called "distributed power"—the notion of co-creation, of sharing our role in the information system with users.

I tried to draw the librarians a picture of what I imagined: "In a world of distributed power, the [traditional] top-down pyramid becomes a geodesic grid. You replace the dumb terminal or television set with a telecomputer that can be a video screen, processor, and communications device all in one. Then you hook it up to all the other computers in the world and serve that network with fiber-optic connections offering nearly unlimited bandwidth..."

The top-bottom metaphor I described is well worn by now but it seemed like a revolutionary insight at the time. Throughout history, it posited, power had been arranged in a hierarchal pyramid where the intelligence (and thus power) resided at a central location and was distributed downward for consumption. At a television station or newspaper that pattern was obvious: we learned things and then passed them along, as we saw fit, to the audience. The same was true even of online services in those days: huge mainframe computers hosting databanks that were accessed over telephone connections by personal computers that were essentially just dumb terminals. I even argued that the model of a huge central government putting citizens on its fringes represented the same "smart on top, dumb on the bottom" system. Yet I sensed this was changing quickly, and I told the librarians:

The exciting new concept here is...the sense of distributed power and interactive communication. The consumer becomes a user or participant and can add to the grid as well.

My experience is that this marks a fundamental shift in expectation. Not only does connection change the volume and speed of information transfer, it also changes what you expect from information.

If you use E-mail for a while, postal mail seems unbearably slow.

If I grow accustomed to accessing Vu-Text (an early news archive) at 11:30 Thursday night, a closed library seems unacceptable.

This is the lesson everybody in the information business must decipher and incorporate...Like nearly everybody else, I examine this equation with a combination of awe and trepidation: what will the future bring? What if we guess wrong? Will I have to retrain? Can I keep up?

But the other half of the equation gives me greater comfort: the quality of information gets to be more and more important, and that's what we have been doing best all along.

Yes, I am proud of the insights I articulated in the early stages of the digital revolution. I saw and predicted the coming changes in news about as accurately as anybody I know, developing a clear early understanding of the fundamental ways in which the networked world would change our relationship with information.

So why didn't I do more about it? That's a question that troubles me still.

It wasn't like I was some Old Testament prophet crying lamentations in the wilderness. I was a newspaper editor and later corporate news executive working for smart people and a company I respected. I had far more opportunity to change things than most people.

Thinking about this ceaselessly has yielded a long list of possibilities but no comprehensive answer.

Certainly I suffered from incrementalism. Even in areas where I could have instituted change on my own initiative, often I was too often deferential to the established order, to the traditions and professional ideologies I'd grown up with. I wrote blog posts of genuine urgency, but didn't do enough to follow through.

I also lacked confidence in my understanding of business issues and was unable to argue authoritatively about such issues as balancing the erosion of existing revenues against the need to establish beachheads in emerging opportunities. I didn't understand business processes well enough to see why advertising sales staffs would be as stubborn as newsroom curmudgeons in resisting fundamental change.

I also recognize now that probably nothing could have altered the fundamental process of disruption the industry since has endured—certainly there was nothing I could have done. The "creative destruction of capitalism" we've now seen close up is, indeed, destructive. Braver decisions and quicker changes might have mitigated the damages, perhaps even changed the slope of the curve, but in the end the large, successful enterprises of one era could not morph painlessly into another.

There is much to criticize in my performance and that of the news industry generally, but a great deal of the carping hindsight that passes for analysis today is just bunk.

"If only" newspapers had invented Craigslist. "If only" newsrooms had embraced video sooner. "If only…"

Think about that. How could inventing Craigslist—a rudimentary way to give away classified adds—have saved a single newsroom job? Craig Newmark and friends turned more than $100 billion in newspaper advertising revenue into something like $100 million in revenue for Craigslist by giving away most ads. Newspapers could have given away advertising, I suppose, but "inventing" Craigslist wouldn't have saved that $99.9 billion difference.

Video? It has indeed emerged as one of a dozen useful initiatives that help in moving away from print-only operations, but even now isn't a meaningful revenue engine. Even YouTube, backed by mighty Google, only recently became modestly profitable, according to the best estimates. Indeed, newspapers diving into video before widespread broadband in their markets surely would have wasted more money than they made.

Despite many failures and widespread newsroom carnage, I remain convinced that the foundations of tomorrow's information order will be rooted in the traditions and disciplines of our best journalism—that high-quality news is simply more valuable than unverified or casually accumulated information, and that markets will evolve to reward that.

Some of our leading news organizations will weather this transition and comprise the framework for providing that valuable, quality product. Others will not.

I have no patience with people who will not see this in its full complexity, particularly critics who stand outside the fray and sneer. It doesn't matter how smart they are; in the end their performance amounts to cheap self-gratification that does little to advance the cause.

A McClatchy board member asked me some years ago what I thought was the biggest change "the internet" had brought to newsrooms.

It took me a moment to sort through the possible answers, for there are many. One might be the introduction of the always-on, twenty-four-hour news cycle that made our old notions of the newspaper as "a daily miracle" seem quaint. Another huge change is the availability of so many new tools, allowing print newsrooms to employ video, for example, database journalism, and techniques like non-linear storytelling.

However, I settled on another: the total erosion of the gate-keeper model of news.

I understand the gatekeeper's role intimately; I practiced it for decades. In Anchorage I put a lot of stories in the paper that powerful people wanted to keep out—and I excluded quite a few that staffers wanted to put in, as well. I took my responsibility seriously enough to lose both sleep and stomach lining, and I believe I served readers in Alaska well.

So what? The ability to distribute information exploded exponentially and soon outran all our old conventions. I told editors in McClatchy they could remain at the gates if they wished, but they were going to look pretty silly. The fences have all come down, and all the people are now roaming around somewhere over there.

Gates can't work. Today's news environment instead requires editors with other tools and new insights about how to help improve the quality of information for their readers. I often cite the logic of an old-time, circuit-riding country preacher who explained why he always traveled with a piano player: "Son, I can't convert 'em until I get 'em in the tent."

The editors and news executives who never even tried to understand—whose antagonistic resistance to almost every change made newsroom transitions so much harder—did tremendous damage to their profession. Ignorance is one thing; willful, self-interested delusion is another. Shame on them.

Chapter Twenty
Thirsty

Honestly, I don't think I could have made it to age thirty-five if I hadn't been drinking—and I'm certain I wouldn't have made it much farther if I hadn't quit.

Alcohol was a defining characteristic of my early years in newspapers. Alcohol and a few other drugs filled a large part of the experimental middle period. And much to my surprise, sobriety became the theme of the competitive successes and accomplishments that followed.

Today I can see my early drunken years were at least partly self-medication, though at the time I thought I was drinking simply because it was fun and made life feel better. Alcohol made dull circumstances more interesting, smoothed ragged edges of insecurity, and built bonds with a larger cadre of talented, likable drinkers.

In rough-and-tumble Alaska, a barroom often was the anteroom to pleasures waiting beyond: an upstairs room for smoking pot, a downstairs gambling parlor, the company of a dancer still sprinkled with glitter after her work was done. All were ubiquitously available in Anchorage, always lubricated with alcohol. A drinker's reputation was the ticket for admission.

While our circumstances in those days actually were romantic, they were nowhere nearly as romantic as my imagination. For me, the drinking life put embroidery on ordinary experiences to dress them up as grand adventures. So what if I was covering crime or city politics in a small, out-of-the-way town somewhere north of nowhere? In my mind, the romance and wonder with which I engaged those struggles gave them the texture and patina of Mark Twain's gold-rush stories, peopled them with Damon Runyon characters like Harry The Horse and the Seldom Seen Kid. It was all lit up from within by the warm glow of Jimmy Breslin's Manhattan saloons.

Later I would wonder how much of what I perceived was real and how much simply an artifact of invention, but finally I realized: it was all real, of course. What else is a writing life but experience filtered through imagination? Could those Runyonesque characters have roamed Broadway without Damon Runyon's stories? Did Marvin the Torch "build vacant lots" without the Breslin columns?

From the start I enjoyed the capacity and enthusiasm of a natural drinker, skipping quickly through the apprentice phase between rookie and regular by virtue of determined and steady practice. Between divorce from my Mormon wife in 1974 and my last drink eleven years later I drank on far more days than I abstained, usually under control—by my own rather flexible standards—but often and increasingly to excess, even by my own lights. Over those years I worked through a thousand hangovers and sometimes drove myself home by closing one eye and leaning out an open window. I broke my promises as often as the traffic laws. I was a well-meaning menace, one of a thousand who roamed the nights in Anchorage in those years, a good-time guy whose selfishness, in the end, knew no bounds.

Do I need to mention that my second marriage also suffered? Looking back I'm astonished that it was strong enough to stand those strains until I'd had enough. I wasn't a mean or foul-tempered drunk, I didn't get caught driving blitzed, and I rarely missed work, but I acted like the nights belonged to me alone.

When I was two or three martinis in, other obligations either dimmed or disappeared and I was focused mainly on preserving, maybe enhancing, that buzz. Often, especially in early days, I did;

I'd hit a steady rhythm of drinking and pleasure where each fueled the other, a self-sustaining cycle that could last for quite a long time. Inevitably that pattern shifted. By the time I quit the days of good times lubricated by alcohol were increasingly rare. What I wanted, almost always, was more. No matter where else I was supposed to be or when I'd promised to be home, the embrace of the barroom more often prevailed.

I took my last drink at an all-night private party in a fancy home near the ocean in South Anchorage in the early-morning hours of Friday, September 13, 1985. I pulled over to the shoulder of a deserted highway not long after I left the party to vomit it all up, kneeling beside my bright red Saab in a light rain. By the time I pulled into our driveway on Government Hill at four or five in the morning I'd have argued I was sober again. Whatever; I was painfully clearheaded.

I dreaded the coming conversation with Barb, not so much afraid of what would be said as disheartened because I knew precisely what it would be. I could have played either side in the argument to come, having rehearsed the roles so many times before. I would try in a dozen ways to say "I'm sorry" but I wouldn't even believe it myself.

I sat for a long time alone at our dining room table, full of guilt, disgusted with myself. How could I say I wouldn't ever do it again? I knew I would. I'd made and broken so many similar promises.

I always truly intended to do what I promised, but in clearer moments I knew this couldn't go on, that Barbara couldn't be expected to believe I'd change, especially when things just kept getting worse.

I wasn't stupid, just drunk.

I wrote myself a long, self-pitying note acknowledging that I was too weak to change, bemoaning the promise I was throwing away, and then went to bed in the guest room. Barb left for work long before I arose and struggled toward wakefulness the next morning. The house was as quiet and empty as my hopes for the future. I was sick. I'd thrown up so much the night before I couldn't speak, and the note I'd written on my yellow legal tablet was as stark and desperate by daylight as it had been in my foggy pre-dawn some hours before.

For reasons unknown to me still, I decided that this time I'd ask for help finding a way out.

It wasn't because I expected it to work, whatever I thought "work" would mean. My mom had made the same promises and more: she'd checked into a psychiatric hospital, gone to meetings, hung the Serenity Prayer on her bedroom wall, and still died drunk. My dad, whose powerful workingman's constitution kept him on the treadmill a little longer, had rolled his car while drinking three years later and died.

Mom died when she was 46, the week I graduated from college; Dad was 52. I was now almost 35; why would I think things would go differently for me?

I suppose I had concluded at some unconscious level that I couldn't quit alone, so I called the only source of help I knew and asked for a meeting schedule. There was only one at mid-day near my house that Friday, at the downtown YMCA. That wouldn't have been my first choice, for I imagined it populated not by tortured, suffering talents like me but common bums and street drunks. I don't think I believed at any level that attending would help.

Still, I couldn't think of anything else to do, and noon found me in sliding into a metal folding chair on the back row in a meeting room at the Y, a few paces from the auditorium where my mom had dropped me off for much-hated square-dance lessons something like twenty-five years before. Some of the street people I'd expected to see were there, but so were some well-dressed office workers with lunch bags balanced on their laps. The room wasn't full but felt crowded. A thick haze of cigarette smoke hung over a long table in the center of the room. An industrial strength coffee urn steamed away in one corner.

I remember little with specificity about the hour I spent there, certainly nothing about any steps or promises or slogans. I do remember an attractive young Yupik woman in a pink dress who sat at the head of the table and, after the ritual readings and greetings, began to tell her gruesome story in a soft, articulate voice.

She said she'd been a street drunk on Fourth Avenue, an area I knew well from nights I sometimes ended in the sleazy bars clustered together there. She'd traded sex with GIs from the Air Force base for six-packs of Oly beer, she told us straightforwardly. She'd slept in dumpsters in the alley.

None of the stories surprised me. Hearing them from a pretty, well-dressed young woman at noontime in downtown Anchorage did.

Later it occurred to me that the first seeds of hope might have planted that Friday, but I certainly had no clear notion of it at the time. My head was full of cotton and fog, my heart full of remorse. I was still sick, I still couldn't speak, and I still dreaded the inevitable conversation yet to come when Barb got home from work. But I had done something new. I'd gone to a meeting. That felt different.

Barb didn't bring up my escapade from the night before when she came home; surely she was as sick of the predictable argument as I. When I gathered the momentum to say something about it, I told her what I'd done at the YMCA. She said something mildly affirmative, but her eyes reflected little optimism.

I went back to the Y at noon every day for a month. After a week or two somebody mentioned that there were other meetings around town; I guess I knew that, but this was the place I'd found first. I hadn't made any declarations, but I hadn't had a drink in, what, two weeks? Then three?

I read the book they gave me and underlined parts that seemed to have been written just for me. I wrote notes on the blank pages at the back until they were full. I'd learned all about underlining and note-taking; after all, I was a college boy. I kept a painfully personal journal, too, mainly recording impressions of the various meetings and sketches to remind me of the personalities I'd encountered. By the end of a month—forty or fifty meetings later—I had filled quite a few pages.

"I want to do this without regard to my intellectual arrogance," I wrote a few days after that first meeting. "I figure I will have to act humble until I learn how to be humble if I want to have a chance at this. And I need the chance."

Later, I wrote, "I now understand one way in which I drank. I excused the excess as okay because it was due me—I work hard, I'm successful, I'm a nice guy. I solve everybody else's problems, so I deserve this."

After a couple of dry weeks Barb and I decided to try going out. We looked at one another as the same question occurred simultaneously to us both: What the hell do you do on Friday night when you don't drink? We ended up bowling a few games at the Elks Club, a place where I doubted we would run into anybody we knew.

We didn't that night, but I knew a lot of people from every stratum of Anchorage society and began to dread running into somebody who would ask me about not drinking or, far worse, about why I was going to all those meetings. When I mentioned this sometime later to an older fellow with some experience he put me straight with a single question: "You didn't mind them watching you throw up on your shoes, but you don't want them to know you're not drinking?"

The first encounter didn't take long. An acquaintance who had been a source on my big heroin series years before approached me at a meeting in the Teamsters Hall one evening, his face all one big smile. "I've been wondering when you'd get here," he said. Soon enough I encountered many others: friends, enemies, rivals; people I liked and people I didn't; people who helped me along and some, doubtless, who sat back waiting for me to fail.

The meetings and the years have unfolded with many shifts and variations since that first tenuous month in Anchorage, but there have been some constants. I never did learn to like bowling, but, as of today, I haven't had a drink.

Chapter Twenty-one
A People in Peril

We sometimes failed to live up to our professional egos and journalistic ideals at the *Daily News*, but the results could be spectacular when we did. There's no better example than the series of stories for which the paper won the 1989 Pulitzer Prize for Public Service—"A People in Peril."

The subject was brutally tragic and profoundly important: beset by cultural engulfment, a generation of young Indians, Eskimos, and Aleuts were killing themselves, often following disastrous alcoholic binges. Other manifestations of their peril were reflected in the grim statistics of child neglect, domestic abuse and other violence. Suicide was more than ten times as likely to claim a young Native male as an average American of similar age.

As the lead article declared, this was truly "Eskimo Armageddon."

For all its consequence, the epidemic was rarely mentioned and wasn't part of the state's public discourse. Aside from racist stereotypes of "drunken Natives" and the heroic but isolated work of a few crusaders, the escalating destruction of Alaska's first societies was hardly ever spoken about. Nowhere was it meaningfully on the public agenda. Although Anchorage, home to about 12,000 Native residents, was the state's "largest Native village," the worst of the destruction took place in regional towns, tiny hamlets, and fish camps in rural Alaska, far from official or general public notice.

For example, in those days the Alaska State Troopers—the only statewide law enforcement across the Alaska's vast regions—did not keep statistics on accidental death or suicide specifically by race or residence. Public health statistics were likewise inadequate; there was no bar graph or official calculation to dramatize or even chart the escalating destruction. Shame, ignorance, indifference, and simple racism all played a role in keeping the gruesome secrets.

Thanks to my wife Barbara Hodgin, I knew far more about the scope of the tragedy than most. In a variety of jobs as a social worker and state employee, she'd traveled to isolated villages scattered all over the state and seen the deterioration and death first hand. More than once she returned from a trip to the Bush in shock over what she'd witnessed.

"Something has to be done," she'd tell me.

Mike Doogan, then a city desk editor, also raised an alarm.

"Do you read the obits and death notices in our paper?" he asked me one day.

"Well, mostly. Sometimes. Why?"

"Take a look at the number of young Native men who show up there," he advised me. "There's something happening."

This wasn't entirely news to any of us. In late 1981 we'd taken note of some of the same patterns and tried to report on the issue, but had come up short in capturing the whole story. As we would learn later, the truths about this situation were buried deep beneath the surface—hidden by the denial and shame alcoholism and suicide bring in all societies, masked by official ignorance or indifference. At that time we weren't up to the task of unearthing them. We finally published a series that raised many of the right questions but offered neither persuasive proof of the problems nor any answers.

That ultimately unsatisfying result then might well have kept us from making a second effort. Newspapers generally hate to repeat reporting they've already done; the rationale "we did a piece on that not long ago" has doomed many a worthy suggestion.

I asked the paper's toughest reporter, Rich Mauer, to take a look and tell me if he thought we ought to try again.

He spent almost a month interviewing people and researching statistics and then sent me a report. It began like this:

"However bad you think this is, it's worse."

The *Daily News* had a larger and more sophisticated newsroom than we'd had when we tackled the subject six years earlier, and Managing Editor Pat Dougherty and I were better equipped as well for the task of managing the effort. With Mauer's scoping memo as our initial guide, we convened an ad hoc team and started planning.

This time we wouldn't stop digging until we knew we'd done all we could. "We may not be able to answer some of these questions, but if that's so I want us to be able to say they're unanswerable, not just that we hadn't found out," I told the staff. If there were holes or errors in our reporting, reflexive denials and ingrained indifference would smother the story once again. It had to be comprehensive and irrefutable.

I also recognized that reporting on these topics would be charged politically and culturally. We were a largely white newspaper staff in the state's largest city and we planned to describe awful truths about brown people who mainly lived in rural villages. With only two exceptions—reporter John Tetpon and editorial writer Martha Upicksoun, both Inupiat—everyone in our newsroom was rooted in the dominant Western culture. Alaska's racial climate and history were no prettier than elsewhere in America, and we knew we would face criticism no matter what. We could only work to make sure we didn't deserve it.

Thus began a painstaking effort that would take more than six months and, at various times, involve more than a third of our ninety-person newsroom. We assigned our best reporters and editors full time and brought in others when needed. Mauer, Sheila Toomey, and Kathleen McCoy would play central roles in writing the stories; Mike Campbell and Richard Murphy spearheaded the work of designing the presentation and adding compelling photojournalism that told a large part of the story on its own. Dougherty organized and ran the project, establishing high standards and helping staffers meet them. Many others deserve recognition as well.

We started simply enough, gathering the basic facts and statistics that official agencies had ignored. There was no official tally of how many Alaska Natives deaths involved alcohol or suicide, so Mauer took several years' worth of press releases from law-enforcement agencies and created a database on his Macintosh to calculate the shocking total. Neither were there Public Health statistics about how big or widespread the suicide epidemic was, so we tallied the numbers and made our own comparisons. For example, we showed that young Native men (the most vulnerable segment) committed suicide at a rate more than ten times greater than the national average for young men. We tried to make the impact of the suicides in one small village real by reminding readers that the same rate in Anchorage would have meant the loss of every student in two of our biggest high schools within two years.

The more we learned, the more determined we became to do this story justice. As the scale of the tragedy unfolded and we began to see patterns and reasons behind it, all of us who were involved realized that doing this right would demand our very best.

That's what we gave it. We assigned staff and devoted time knowing that our decisions meant the rest of the paper would be worse for however long it took. I alerted publisher Grilly that the local news report was going to be thin for a while and told him why. He backed us completely. We traveled tens of thousands of miles across Alaska's expanse, interviewed hundreds of people, and took thousands of photos. That provided all the ingredients we needed to tell the story, but it didn't tell us how to do so.

We'd planned to publish the articles in November 1987, but when the time came we didn't feel quite ready.

So we postponed the series. Because the Christmas season wouldn't have been a good time to capture public attention and keep it focused on such a complex, disturbing disclosures, we didn't run it in December, either. We used the delay to polish the presentation and report even deeper.

Commitment to the effort engulfed our newsroom. Copy editors not assigned to the project volunteered to take home page proofs and give them even closer scrutiny. Writers who weren't otherwise assigned to the project likewise stepped up.

One of the most powerful elements we published emerged during this period: a special stand-alone section called "In Memoriam" with photos and short personal stories about Native people who hadn't gotten much attention when they died. A dozen staffers not involved in the primary reporting volunteered to research individual items, and page after page of individual photos and authentic stories were arresting proof of why this series was important. (I remembered this years later when the *New York Times* employed a similar approach to produce its outstanding "Portraits of Grief" about individual 9-11 victims.)

I took advantage of the delay to do something I had never done with a story before: brief a number of influential Native elders and leaders and some public health officials beforehand about the stories we planned to publish. None was naive about the problem, but as I anticipated some didn't trust us to handle it fairly or in context. I was able to show them how deeply we'd researched the issue and what we'd learned of how enormous the problems were. Beyond that, I could only assure them that we'd do everything possible to show the reasons behind the epidemic and also would highlight whatever solutions or hopeful trends we could identify.

Some Native health professionals embraced our effort from the start. People like Doug Modig, an Indian social worker, were invaluable in helping us not just identify problems but also see them in cultural and historical context. I have come to believe one of our greatest contributions came in explaining how generations of cultural engulfment and disenfranchisement contributed to conditions that bred the epidemic. Despite our best efforts, though, I'm afraid most Alaskans never got beyond the point of seeing it as "a Native problem."

We wanted to get our findings into print before the legislature convened in late January. We were convinced that a broad, systemic response was the only hope for solutions, and we knew that would require legislative attention. (One small specific: once we pointed out that killing a moose out of season could be a felony under Alaska law but bootlegging booze in a dry village was only a misdemeanor, the legislature would move swiftly to correct that.)

We published our first installment on January 10, 1988. Our report unfolded in a sophisticated presentation of more than sixty stories spread over ten days.

I wrote a long front-page essay as an introduction and summary of our findings. It started like this:

> Something is stalking the village people.
>
> Across the state, the Eskimos, Indians and Aleuts of Bush Alaska are dying in astonishing numbers. By suicide, accident and other untimely, violent means, death is stealing the heart of a generation and painting the survivors with despair.
>
> A growing sense of helplessness simmers in alcohol throughout the Bush. Among a growing percentage of Alaska Natives, life has become equal parts violence, disintegration and despair. An epidemic of suicide, murder and self destruction threatens to overwhelm cultures that have for centuries survived and prospered in the harshest environments on earth.
>
> The village of Alakanuk lived on the razor's edge: a town of 550 with eight suicides, dozens of attempts, two murders and four drownings in 16 months. This was Eskimo Armageddon.

On the Sunday we launched the series, the front page was dominated by Sheila Toomey's long narrative telling Alakanuk's story for the first time. To get the story, she'd lived for a while in the village almost 500 miles southwest of Anchorage. She stayed with a pair of nuns; local residents at first were understandably reluctant and sometimes hostile about sharing their tragic stories with an outsider. In addition to her gift for stylish storytelling, Sheila was adept at patiently building relationships with sources. The story she produced was among the most compelling I have ever read:

> ALAKANUK—In March 1985, a young man walked out onto the tundra behind this Yukon River village and carefully, neatly shot himself in the heart. "I guess I've always looked for a reason to do it," said the note near Louie Edmund's body. "And I found it."
>
> The sound of the shot rolled across the flat delta land through the supper time darkness of a cold spring day. It breached the walls and windows of the wooden houses, marking the moment as a beginning, for Louie Edmund began a 15-month suicide epidemic that ended the lives of eight young villagers.

The governor inserted reference to our series into his State of the State address while our stories were still running in the paper. Reactions and some official responses quickly followed. Many things that could be fixed by changing laws were swiftly accomplished. For example, lawmakers quickly made it illegal for urban liquor stores to take remote orders for booze to be delivered by Bush plane, a common dodge to get around local village ordinances against selling alcohol.

We received little of the criticism or denial I had feared. Instead we got hundreds of requests for reprints and quickly reproduced everything in a package of eighty broadsheet pages in eight sections. The Alaska National Guard (an important institution in rural Alaska) and numerous Native health cooperatives bought copies to distribute by the thousands in local areas. *Newsweek* magazine wrote about our findings and helped spread the message even farther; I took one telephone call from a man in Greenland who read it and told me people there were struggling with the same problems.

There was of course no swift end to suicides or drastic reduction in village alcohol abuse. The problems, as we reported, had been generations in the making and it surely would take many years to resolve them. Protecting Native youth in their most vulnerable years, for instance, required programs that educated them years in advance.

We did get criticism from some *Anchorage Times* reporters and a few others who characterized our effort as showboating; a flashy stunt that we must know was destined for futility. "Everybody knows there's nothing you can do about it," a *Times* staffer said at a Press Club function months later.

A reporter from an Anchorage television station quickly made the rebuttal for me: "Well, the *Daily News* did something."

And yes, we did. As I repeated in numerous speeches at service clubs, churches, and other venues, we had done all we could: the part a newspaper could do. Solutions would demand the same from many other institutions and individuals—that each do the part they could do. This was society's problem, and society would have to bring to bear combined efforts from many quarters even to start addressing it.

We had made it impossible to deny the crisis. No excuse remained for ignoring it.

More than a year later the *Daily News* was awarded its second Pulitzer Prize for Public Service for "reporting about the high incidence of alcoholism and suicide among native Alaskans in a series that focused attention on their despair and resulted in various reforms."

Twice in less than fifteen years this small paper in a remote city had captured journalism's biggest prize. This time it came as no surprise to me—partly because I knew how good and important our journalism had been, but specifically because I was tipped off beforehand. C.K. McClatchy was on the Pulitzer board that year, and while he had to excuse himself and leave the room during voting on the public service prize, he of course learned that the *Daily News* had won it.

Early on the morning of the vote he'd called to tell me we were a finalist "in category one," meaning public service. Later that day he reported simply that "the board has done the true and just thing in category one."

I shared the news with Barbara, whose initial insights were a key motivation for our inquiry, and Dougherty, the project's key editor who was away at Harvard University on a prestigious, year-long Nieman Fellowship. Advance knowledge of the award meant Dougherty had time to slip back into town for the public announcement March 31 and gave me time to have a bunch of celebratory t-shirts printed and ready for the event. As it had for Kay Fanning in 1975, the public announcement came first by phone—a call I arranged to find me in the middle of the newsroom where I could share the moment with the astonishingly talented staff that had contributed mightily to the effort.

Dougherty, once a good and frequent poker player, met his future wife at Harvard that year and told me later on the night before their wedding that he'd become anxious when he heard he Pulitzer news. "I've always believed luck comes in streaks, good luck and bad," he said. "After winning the fellowship, meeting K.J. and getting our Pulitzer all in one year, I thought maybe I ought to spend the next year under my bed."

Daily News Publisher Kay Fanning introduces the paper's new majority owner, C.K. McClatchy, at an Anchorage Chamber of Commerce luncheon in 1979. His family-owned company, California-based McClatchy Newspapers, bought eighty percent interest in the *News* and later purchased the remaining interest as well. McClatchy's determination, fighting spirit, and deep pockets added up to a crucial turning point in the Great Alaska Newspaper war, though at the time few thought the *News* could win it.

Jerry Grilly, shown here addressing an all-hands meeting at the *Daily News*, had never worked for a daily newspaper when he was hired to run the paper's operations, first as general manager and later as publisher. His combination of competitive vigor, strategic sense, and intuitive leadership were crucial to victory for the paper he led from hopeless underdog to sole survivor in the Great Alaska Newspaper War. He later achieved victory in another head-to-head newspaper competition in Denver, Colorado.

Robert B. Atwood, the *Anchorage Times* owner and publisher, dominated Alaska media and Anchorage society for decades. Described by *New Yorker* writer John McPhee as "a big, friendly, old-football-tackle sort of a man" he was by turns charming and ruthless in pursuing his vision of Alaska. He sold his newspaper in 1989, about two and one-half years before it folded.

We embraced a different metaphor in describing our ambitions in the community, declaring that we wanted the paper to become "the tribal fire around which Alaskans gathered to tell the stories that defined themselves as a people." Alaskans feel a fierce sense of place and we did all we could to incubate and satisfy that impulse. The stated desire was that every edition of the paper would be instantly recognizable as an Alaska publication, and our pages were replete with stories of wilderness adventures, wildlife antics and events like the Iditarod sled dog race and the annual wild, scrambling race to the top of Mount Marathon. Staff cartoonist Peter Dunlap-Shohl designed this logo, which I used on certificates recognizing staffers who served this mission especially well.

The *Daily News* also pioneered using personal computers—in our case, always Macs—to assist in journalism. In 1985 reporter Richard Mauer (shown here with Dee Boyles and me at one of our early Macs) worked with freelancer Larry Makinson to build a database of campaign contributions that led to important revelations. *Time* magazine recognized it in an article entitled, "New Paths to Buried Treasure: Computers are revolutionizing investigative journalism."

The state legislature convened hearings after the *Daily News* broke the story of a critical grand jury that called for impeachment of Governor Bill Sheffield in 1985. We flooded the story with a team of reporters unlike any Alaska news organizations had fielded before. Shown here at a Sheffield press conference during the hearings are *ADN* photographer Michael Penn, Alaska Public Radio's Peter Kenyon and, looking away from the camera at the far left, *ADN* reporters Sheila Toomey and Stan Jones.

An aggressive champion of open government and freedom of information, the *Daily News* sued the Alaska Legislature in 1986 for crafting the state budget in secret meetings. It was big news when we won, reported here by the *Juneau Empire*, effectively stopping further legislative action. The paper's longtime attorney, D. John McKay, pictured above, had come through for us yet again. The Alaska Supreme Court later ruled that courts didn't have the constitutional right to regulate legislative actions, but by then our point had been made.

By June, 1986 the *Anchorage Daily News* was winning its war against the *Times*, having established a growing circulation lead and capturing the lion's share of advertising. Though it was not yet profitable, mainly due to cheap rates and discounts mandated by competition, the path to victory was apparent and McClatchy built a $30 million headquarters for the paper on Northway Drive in Mountain View. It represented a highly visible symbol of confidence in the paper's future as well as a huge quality of life improvement for about four hundred employees.

Key staffers flew to New York City with me aboard the McClatchy corporate jet to attend the Columbia University luncheon where the 1989 Pulitzers were awarded. Here at a celebration afterward are, from left, Richard Mauer, Pat Dougherty, Sheila Toomey, and Mike Campbell.

This is the Gold Medal awarded by the Pulitzer Board in the Public Service category. It's the only category that gets a medal—and the only one that comes without a cash prize. Winners in other categories now receive $10,000.

On June 3, 1992 Anchorage had two thick, colorful daily newspapers, both shown here announcing the folding of the *Anchorage Times* on their front pages. The next morning, only the *Daily News* was left, a signal change in Alaska media and, as it turned out, in my career. Three years later I, too, was gone from Alaska.

At the time of its folding, the *Times* was ending a run that involved many of the best journalists in its history. Frequent clashes between journalistic purposes and management's prerogatives made many of those tenures short, and I believe I outlasted seven different *Times* editors. One was Drex Heikes, who was raised in Anchorage and after leaving led the *Las Vegas Sun* to a Public Service Pulitzer and did noteworthy work at the *Los Angeles Times* and elsewhere. From the left at a farewell roast for him are Don Byron, Danny Baum, David Predeger, Ellis E. Conklin, Heikes, and E.W. Piper.

Chapter Twenty-two
A journalistic oil slick

B arb and I were on vacation in the red rock canyons of Utah in March, 1989 when Captain Joe Hazelwood and Exxon's supertanker fetched up against Bligh Reef and unloosed a flood of crude oil into one of the world's richest and most productive marine environments. Rushing home, the extent of the disaster became apparent when our Alaska Airlines flight descended across Prince William Sound toward Anchorage.

We were flying first class, surrounded by prosperous-looking men in expensive clothes whom I took to be oil executives or spill contractors of one sort or another. They mostly seemed unmoved by the spreading portrait of disaster outside our windows, some of them hardly even interested. I was sick to my stomach and sick at heart.

As sickening as it was, the panorama from 15,000 feet was no preparation for the awful reality that awaited us on the shoreline. If you never have seen a major crude oil spill, you cannot imagine it.

Perhaps you envision rainbow hues of gasoline spreading behind an outboard motor and quickly evaporating from the water's surface. Try instead to picture thick, smothering blankets of oil frothed by churning tides and turned all shades of brown and black, the smell itself an overpowering and inescapable presence. As thick crude washes ashore and stacks up in tide pools and estuaries, it sometimes becomes knee deep, obviously, and self-evidently a killer, destroying everything it touches.

And it was touching everything.

Readers responded most emotionally to photos of blackened seabirds and choking, brown-eyed otters awash in the fatal tides, as of course they would. In truth, though, devastation was everywhere, often hidden from view by the crude oil that gushed unchecked from the ruptured tanker by the millions of gallons, day after painful day. The environment around Native villages that had sheltered and supported residents for generations suddenly became a dead zone. The fishing industry that provided thousands of livelihoods from Cordova to Yakutat vanished in a few hours; the once-rich fishing grounds become a killing field instead.

The *Daily News* had responded to news of the spill far more professionally than many oil industry and regulatory authorities. By the time I got home the paper had already deployed with speed and practiced expertise to do its job, chronicling the devastation and displaying the results for all to see. Finding no suitable boats available for charter, the newsroom bought a fast, sturdy Boston Whaler, named it The Muckraker, and set out.

Soon the state was awash in journalists from every corner of the globe, but the *Daily News* was there before their arrival and long after they left, and nobody told the story better. For a long time there was little besides oil-spill stories on our front page, and it was months before a day passed without some substantial presence on A-1. The story of our Pulitzer Prize did make it onto the front page; it ran with a two-column head at the bottom. That day's banner was: "NTSB: Captain too drunk to run ship."

Unimaginably, the first reaction at the *Anchorage Times* was to downplay the unfolding disaster. Its coverage over the coming days and months would demonstrate quite clearly why the oil industry loved the paper—and why it feared what might happen as the *Daily News* assumed the *Times'* old mantle as "Alaska's Largest Paper."

"The first reaction, of course, will be one of wailing and gnashing of teeth," the *Times'* lead editorial said the day after the spill.

The paper began offering excuses for the oil industry, suggesting that damages wouldn't be as bad as alarmist environmentalists were claiming, noting at one point that the clean-up "will take some days to complete... ."

"One inevitable consequence of the incident will be adverse headlines around the world and the renewal in the fury of the environmental lobbies against any kind of development—and particularly oil development—in Alaska," the paper noted. "Sad to say, this is precisely what some of the groups have been waiting for and hoping for all these long years."

How stupid and insulting that last line was. Many of us certainly had feared such a disaster and some of us had been warning about it for years, but describing it as a hoped-for result was a new low, even for the *Times*.

Less than a week after the catastrophic spill, the *Times* was ready to move on. "It's time to end all the hand-wringing and weeping over the Prince William Sound oil spill," it wrote on March 30. "It's not time now for finger-pointing and oil company bashing. There's been more than enough wails and lamenting and we-told-you-so's from the professional environmentalists."

Within weeks of the spill, Exxon named Bill Allen's Veco International—a home-grown Alaska company—as lead contractor in running the cleanup, a massive effort that ultimately would present Exxon with about $750 million in bills and Veco with $30-40 million in profits. The company hired about 10,000 temporary workers, chartered almost every seaworthy boat in the region, and moved logistical mountains in mounting a cleanup effort that was ubiquitously visible if not actually environmentally successful.

Instead of examining and lamenting the disaster, just a month later, on April 27, Atwood's *Times* was applauding the payday:

Every cloud has a silver lining, they say. And that's certainly true of the oil spill.

Prince William Sound was soiled five weeks ago, and the crude from the tanker Exxon Valdez spread a terrible pall over springtime in Alaska.

But the resulting cleanup effort has produced the biggest economic bonanza in Southcentral Alaska since the height of the pipeline construction a decade and a half ago. Certainly not since the collapse of oil prices and the onset of the big recession four years ago has the economy had such a positive jolt.

Veco's big profits from that work would affect the *Daily News* almost as much as they did Bill Allen. About nine months after Exxon's supertanker hit the reef, Alaskans were stunned to hear that Robert Atwood, the iconic grand old man of Alaska journalism, had sold his venerable, family-owned *Times* to oil-man Allen.

Allen and company wasted no time in announcing their intentions: "It's War," one *Times* headline proclaimed in describing their competitive intentions toward the *Daily News*. We happily enlarged that and posted it prominently in the newsroom as we buckled down for what everybody knew would be a bare-knuckled fight to the finish.

At first Veco did a lot of competitive things right, and it did them quickly: doubling the local reporting staff, searching for professional editors, and moving publication from afternoon to "all day," which meant mostly morning. The new editors moved quickly to redesign the paper's outdated format, increased color photography, and expanded syndicated features and comics.

Despite what I viewed as its many continuing sins, during this era the *Anchorage Times* practiced the most honest journalism of its history. The paper hired skilled, professional editors like Drew Heikes (like me, a local boy) and Fred Dickey, though neither would last long under the oppressive demands of the owners. I believe I once calculated that I outlasted seven different *Times* editors during my ten-year run as the boss.

Many of the energetic and productive reporters they brought aboard in those days were good enough to cause some anxiety and even envy at the *News*. One response? I hired a lot of them.

All their improvements were obviously expensive; what worried us most was that they didn't seem to care. Writing about Allen's *Exxon Valdez* profits in October 1990, the *Alaska Business Monthly* said "the entire cache [has been] set aside to acquire and upgrade the newspaper ... Allen believes the *Times* is positioned to win what could be the last great newspaper war in the United States."

I can imagine a couple of reasons why Bill Allen didn't worry overmuch about his expenses at that point.

Most important, I believe he always saw that the *Times*' biggest value was the way he could use it to be helpful to the major oil companies that provided the vast bulk of his annual nine-figure revenues. The paper's steadfast support for Big Oil acted like a loss leader that kept oil company doors open to Veco—and that kept the big money flowing. So what if they lost $5-10 million a year on the newspaper? Veco was making more than $100 million annually at that point.

Years later, an elaborate multi-year FBI investigation would produce telephone tapes and Juneau hotel videos proving how brutally corrupt Allen and Veco were willing to be on behalf of oil interests. Good will from the oil industry was basically priceless to Allen.

As an article in the *Chicago Tribune* put it, Bill Allen "could be likened to press barons of the past who bought newspapers as platforms for their views." A newspaper once run by Colonel Robert McCormick, as the *Tribune* was, ought to know.

Still, the costs escalated, and nobody (especially a rich man perhaps) likes to lose money. "It's a tougher fight than I thought when I went into it," Allen told the business monthly in the fall of 1990. "I didn't know anything about a newspaper."

He did know this: he wouldn't have to fight the Alaska newspaper war alone.

Within months, Big Oil and other Alaska business heavy-weights would begin to rally around the *Times*. The paper clearly needed their help.

By then we'd established a commanding lead among Anchorage readers. Audit Bureau of Circulations reports from 1989 showed the *Daily News* with daily circulation of about 56,000 against 32,000 for the *Times*; on Sunday, we had a circulation of 72,000 to their 41,000.

Both newspapers were doing what comes naturally in competition: discounting subscription prices, selling cut-rate advertising, and energetically marketing their papers. But Bill Allen and his oil industry pals went much farther.

To help pump up advertising, Arco started secretly paying for ads in the *Times* promoting local non-profit organizations, from Big Brothers to the local homeless shelter. The charities were offered a deal they could not refuse: Arco paid an ad agency for professional designs and then bought big ads in the *Times*—and *only* in the *Times*.

I talked about the covert financing and waved around copies of some of the ads in a speech to the Farthest North Press Club in Fairbanks:

"You'll notice that ARCO's name appears nowhere on these ads, which helps to give the *Times* the appearance of a much broader advertising base than it actually has. It also obscures the fact that there is even more oil money in the Veco *Times* than you might already have suspected.

"This is no small-time program. In the month of December, for example, ARCO purchased more than 49 full pages worth of these ads. Even last month—in February, which is not a tradition-ally heavy advertising season—ARCO paid for 39 full pages. At that rate, ARCO could become the biggest advertiser in the mar-ket—bigger than Sears or J.C. Penney's or Carrs grocery—without even putting their name on a single ad."

We looked at published rates for ads in the *Times* and cal-culated that at the December rate the campaign would have been worth more than $500,000 a year to the *Times*. As it turned out, the campaign petered out a few months later.

Real advertising, however, relies on real circulation, and the *Times* had problems there as well. Rather than counting only readers who actually bought the *Times* each day, Allen's friends colluded to purchase thousands of additional papers each day for their employees, allowing the *Times* to pad its reported circulation.

Solid evidence of the scheme soon made its way into our hands. Unocal (the former Union Oil Company) sent a memo to employees bluntly explaining why the company was buying them subscriptions: "The *Anchorage Times* is very supportive of the oil industry activities in Alaska."

"To keep you apprised of the issues, candidates, and election activities, we are offering all employees a complimentary subscription to the *Anchorage Times*," BP Exploration wrote. The natural gas company also was on board: "The *Times* recently approached us proposing Enstar offer subscriptions to its employees as a way to increase circulation," its memo said. So they did.

Within months, the *Times* featured glowing, business-cover profiles called "Key Players" that just happened to feature executives whose firms had ponied up for subscriptions.

The payoff was even bigger for BP. Before Alaska's August 1990 primary election, the *Times* decided not to produce a traditional informational voters' guide on its own: unbelievably, it simply inserted a copy of BP's own guide for its employees into every copy of its Sunday paper.

"No bias slips into its pages. It's all straightforward data," the paper assured its readers.

You could not say the same about the *Times* coverage of oil industry activities, however; plenty of bias slipped in there.

Sometimes it was as crude as running Exxon PR photos as news pictures illustrating oil spill coverage. In other cases, its service to the industry was more elaborate and extensive.

The most celebrated example came when Congress held hearings in November 1991 to inquire into charges that the industry had illegally attempted to entrap and smear a leading critic. As the *Washington Post* reported, the *Daily News*, "like most major papers, focused on a covert campaign by Alyeska Pipeline Service Co. that included creating a phony environmental group, secretly taping conversations with industry critic Charles Hamel, going through Hamel's garbage, and targeting a congressman for investigation."

Anchorage Times business writer Bert Tarrant, dispatched to Washington especially for the hearings, saw things differently. "Alyeska hearing scorches Hamel," said the paper's page-one banner headline, and Tarrant's first paragraph began, "Oil industry critic Charles Hamel was characterized as an extortionist ... witnesses said Tuesday during congressional testimony."

The *Post*'s media reporter, Howard Kurtz, took note of the wildly divergent stories from Anchorage and summed it up like this: "The *Times* piece resembled [a pipeline company] legal brief." In our paper, columnist Mike Doogan characterized the situation more colorfully, writing, "The *Times* has carried Alyeska's water as faithfully as Gunga Din ... Whatever you do, don't mistake The *Anchorage Times* for a newspaper."

The *Times*' embrace of an all-oil-all-the-time agenda was important and newsworthy in Alaska and we missed few opportunities expose it and brand the paper as "the Veco *Times*," but I thought this particular spat had gone far enough. I wrote a memo to all staffers encouraging calmer tempers, invoking what I called "the Doogan Pig Wrestling Rule," which held, "Never wrestle with a pig. You get all muddy and the pig just has a good time."

"We have made our point, and any genuine examination of the coverage will support us. There is nothing to be gained from name-calling; prolonging this phase of the debate is pointless," I wrote to the staff. "The *Daily News* is the classy operation in this deal. Please ensure that we behave that way."

Generally, we did, although not long before we had failed our professional responsibilities badly with the worst mistake of my professional career, ushering in one of my most ignominious experiences.

We'd received word of bribery going on in the award of contracts for the *Exxon Valdez* spill cleanup—hardly a shocking possibility, given the turmoil, the magnitude of the effort, and the character of some of the people involved. Now we had a witness willing to go on the record telling of bribery he'd witnessed; we also had a collection of boat-sale transaction records our team thought supported his story.

Somehow a bankrupt, convicted arsonist had set himself up leasing boats during the *Exxon Valdez* cleanup, going from nowhere to more than $3 million in business almost overnight. Now we'd tracked down and talked to a former employee who said he saw his boss hand an envelope stuffed with hundred-dollar bills to a key logistics chief working for Veco's cleanup effort.

ADN always worked hard to avoid using anonymous sources, and this witness was identified and talking on the record. Our reporter and editors checked the documents regarding the sale of the boat involved in that transaction and believed they corroborated his story, which was published on April 7, 1991.

We soon would learn that we were horribly wrong. Of course we'd recognized beforehand that writing a story accusing one of our competitor's executives of bribery on the spill project would be especially incendiary, but somehow that hadn't translated into even routine care let alone extra care in evaluating the documentation.

Reaction from Veco and the executive we named was an instantaneous and predictably outraged denial. I issued a "we-stand-by-the-story" reply, but their complaints and protestations escalated; they weren't behaving like guilty people who got caught.

We decided to reevaluate and I asked our best investigative reporter, Richard Mauer—who had not been involved in the story—to backtrack over the work done by other staffers. His reading of the documents we'd partially relied on quickly established the original reporter's interpretation was suspect; things hadn't necessarily happened in the sequence we reported, and indeed the chronology outlined by the documents could be read as pointing toward someone other than the Veco employee.

Still, we had an on-the-record eyewitness, didn't we? At this point our lawyer John McKay took over the internal investigation and dispatched Mauer on a twelve-hundred-mile roundtrip to talk to the source. When he reported back, the wheels came completely off our accusatory story.

As Richard remembers his interview with the story's primary source:

"[The source] got to the part about the envelope stuffed with cash when I stopped him. Would he be able to pick out the guy who was bribed from pictures of the Veco guy and the Exxon guy?

"He wasn't sure.

"Was he sure it was the Veco guy who was bribed, or could it have been the Exxon guy?

"He didn't know. Just as likely to be one or the other, he said. He knows there was an envelope, the sleazy boat guy told him how much was in the envelope, he knows it was handed to someone in authority, but he didn't know which someone it was.

"Trouble is, my memory hasn't been very good since I had all those electroshocks."

"Electroshocks?"

"Yeah, they gave them to me in the prison in Illinois. Fifty-six of them. Memory ain't worth a damn since then."

"You were in prison in Illinois?"

"Yeah, they sent me there because they couldn't control me in the Anchorage jail."

"You were in jail in Anchorage?"

"Yeah. You guys had me on the front page of your paper when I led a prison riot."

"You led a prison riot in the Anchorage jail?"

"Yeah, they couldn't control me."

"Did you tell any of this to [the reporter]?"

"No. He never asked."

At this point, Veco knew its guy wasn't guilty but it had no idea how wrong our newspaper had been—or, thank God, why. I had nightmares in which I watched this guy telling stories of electroshocks and prison riots on the witness stand. I asked McKay to do whatever it took to get us a quick settlement before Veco's lawyers found the guy.

Meanwhile I was sick with worry. What to do? Was there any way to finesse this, or get away lightly? Was there any interpretation that minimized our mistakes or mitigated the errors? The answer, when it came, was simple and straightforward.

One of the rules I'd been advised to apply in sobriety says "when we were wrong [we] promptly admitted it." Well, we were wrong. The answer was to promptly admit it.

I told Veco we had learned that the story was wrong and that we were going to admit that. Yes, on the front page, where the original accusatory story had run.

I told them I was sorry. Bill Allen wanted me to come around and tell people personally, face to face, so I did. It was humiliating and it hurt, but I deserved it.

Then we ran a front-page story headlined "*Daily News* apologizes for reporting bribery charge." It began, "Based on information recently acquired, the *Anchorage Daily News* does not believe an allegation previously reported by it that [a] Veco employee accepted a bribe." It ended noting that the employee and Veco "were pleased with the *Daily News* response and that they accept its apology."

In exchange, McKay had negotiated a release from Veco foregoing legal action, and we never had to tell them the story about the electroshocks. I don't imagine they ever learned.

•••

We were right about the bribery although we were wrong about who took the bribes. Two years later, in the fall of 1993, Exxon executive Bill Alexander pleaded guilty to federal charges that he had accepted "money, ivory, a fur coat, a watch, a truck, and the services of a prostitute during 1989 and 1990" in exchange for steering a boat contract to the boat mogul we'd identified. He was "the other guy" our source's electroshocked mind had been unable to distinguish.

Chapter Twenty-three
In harm's way

The *Times* had always been an oil-industry cheerleader, but under Bill Allen it became a wholly owned subsidiary.

Atwood often bemoaned the fact that his little hometown paper was forced to do battle with a big company from California. Well, we now looked across the trenches and saw much of the global oil industry lined up with our opponent. Though details of the industry's secret advertising underwriting and not-so-secret mass circulation purchases emerged only piecemeal at the time, we had no doubts about the implications.

Lucky for us, we were battle-tested by then. The strategic thinking we'd employed successfully against Atwood's *Times* would be our guide in taking on the Veco *Times*, as well.

Now we were waging war from an advantageous position. "We occupy the high ground here," I wrote in December 1989. "We hold that valuable position because we have fought and paid for it. Our challenge now is to use it to ensure that Veco fights uphill every step of the way.

"Our strategies need not change. The lessons of the last 10 years remain fully in force: allow the competition no free movement; protect our flanks; and respond vigorously to preserve market power at [at least] a 60-40 circulation split ... We believe this new struggle can be shaped by our response. It can either be a 2-3 year fight or a 5-7 year fight, depending on how bloody we can make [these] initial phases."

I repeated a warning we'd issued some years before, when momentum had clearly shifted to us but the outcome remained uncertain: "It would be difficult now to lose, but it would not be hard to fail to win."

In 1987 we noted that *ADN* had achieved many of the benchmarks we'd wanted on the path to victory: we had more circulation than the *Times*, and the gap was growing; we had a lead in advertising share of field and, more important, ad revenue share; readership surveys tilted decisively in our direction, and our quality advantage was undimmed.

Still, we weren't yet profitable and remained worried about a protracted war of attrition that would bleed the leader as well as the loser. "We need to keep the pressure on and be as aggressive as we were on the way up," Stephen Star advised.

In August 1989 we could report two landmark achievements: winning a Pulitzer Prize and posting our first profitable quarter ever under McClatchy ownership, possibly the first in the paper's long subsidized history.

By late 1989 we knew we faced a meaner, far better-financed opponent, and I argued for closing the door on Bill Allen's effort quickly to avoid "the specter of years of continuing a battle of attrition matching us against an opponent financed by the deep pockets of the oil industry..."

Allen is of course their creature," I wrote, "wholly dependent on oil company contracts for existence. That relationship also makes it absurdly easy for oil to finance Allen's newspaper venture if it so desires. Simply adding a couple of profit points to contracts [with Veco] can add up to millions in loose cash for him to spend in the newspaper business...I do not think the major oil companies would spend $30-50 million in a war with us. But I firmly believe they would shuffle some millions to encourage Bill Allen, especially in these early stages where the stakes are highest...

It didn't take long to learn that I was right about that, confirmed by the covert advertising support and wholesale addition of subsidized circulation. I suspect there were additional hidden subsidies we never learned about at all.

By 1990 it was also clear that Bill Allen, like me, wanted to play for a quick knockout. The *Times* was spending lavishly; its oil industry and chamber of commerce buddies had circled the wagons around the paper, and it was gaining on some fronts. It now published an "all-day" paper, having moved principally into a morning cycle like ours; it had matched and in some areas outpaced us on staffing; its newshole was bigger than ours and its competitive response—chasing stories, traveling out of town, using color photography—was vastly improved.

However, the *Times*' gains had not yet translated into meaningful loss for us. Competitive pressure kept circulation and advertising prices low at both papers, so many customers could afford both; it wasn't entirely a zero-sum game.

Yes, it was scary, but I looked at that landscape and saw opportunity. "We are finally focused in a complete head-to-head fight," I wrote in September 1990. "In Vietnam, American commanders yearned for an enemy that would come out of the jungle to fight in the open. Well, our enemy has done that now. And while the *Times* has devoted astonishing money and energy to the fight so far, it's also clear they are operating at the limits of what they can do. A final assault by the *Daily News* in 1991 can deliver decisive blows."

A month later, Jerry Grilly and I made the argument to corporate: "This is the central battle of an eleven-year war, and we want to make it a decisive victory. The *Times* is doing many things right. We need to stifle that."

We'd been fighting the McClatchy phase of this battle for a decade by this time and thinking about it as a war was deeply instinctual for many of us. I'll admit that I probably responded to the appeal of military metaphors more than most, having been a long-time fan of military historian John Keagan and inveterate collector of military quotes and stories.

Frank McCulloch, a fighting Marine in World War II and Korea and a correspondent during Vietnam, may have been first to introduce martial vocabulary early in the struggle.

We recognized at one session that while we could not control what our opponent did, we could and must make sure that none of its important initiatives went unanswered. Consistent with its general arrogance, the *Times* tended to ignore improvements or initiatives at *ADN*; we decided that we would copy immediately anything they did that seemed to be working to keep them from gaining momentum while we implemented our own plans. No matter what they did, we would always respond.

"The Marines would call this 'No free movement across terrain.' We want them to bleed for every inch they advance," McCulloch said. That became a catch phrase in newsroom conversations. Debating whether Plan X was worth doing, somebody would inevitably say, "No free movement across terrain," and then we'd buckle down and do it.

Somewhere along the line I'd clipped and saved a short item from *Harper's* Magazine that summarized strategic advice from the U.S. Army Field Manual. It proved a useful reference again and again in our fight, and I recommend it to anybody planning competitive strategy:

1. CHOICE OF OBJECTIVE: Every military operation should be directed toward clearly defined, decisive, and obtainable objectives.

2. TAKING THE OFFENSIVE: Seize, retain, and exploit the initiative.

3. MASSING OF FORCES: Concentrate combat power at the decisive place and time.

4. ECONOMY OF FORCE: Allocate minimum essential combat power to secondary efforts.

5. EFFECTIVENESS OF MANEUVER: Place the enemy in a position of disadvantage through the flexible application of combat power.

6. SURPRISE: Strike the enemy at a time and/or place and in a manner for which he is unprepared.

7. SIMPLICITY: Prepare clear, uncomplicated plans and clear, concise orders to insure thorough understanding."

I also read a translation of the Sun Tzu classic, *The Art of War*, at some point and quickly distilled two pages of aphorisms I used in thinking about our business strategies. They included:

... If the enemy is taking his ease, harass him; if quietly encamped, force him to move; if well supplied with food, starve him out. Appear at points the enemy must hasten to defend; march swiftly to places where you are not expected.

... The art of war teaches us to rely not on the likelihood of the enemy's not coming, but on our own readiness to receive him; not on the chance of his not attacking, but rather on the fact that we have made our position unassailable.

... There are roads that must not be followed, towns that must not be besieged ... No town should be attacked which, if taken, cannot be held, or if left alone, will not cause any trouble.

... Never forget: When your weapons are dulled, your ardor dampened, your strength exhausted and your treasure spent, other chieftains will spring up to take advantage of your extremity.

Though he wrote hundreds of years before the birth of Christ, Sun Tzu's advice seemed easy to interpret in the context of our commercial struggle: speed, deception, preparation, and constant vigilance all came into play. It was harder to follow his admonition about prudence and restraint, about "towns that must not be besieged." Our initial impulse was always more like John Paul Jones, who told his Navy superiors, "I have no interest in any ship that does not sail fast, for I intend to go in harm's way."

That wasn't my only favorite from the naval hero of the Revolutionary War. Also applicable, it seemed to me, was his later admonition against delay and caution: "... in human affairs the sources of success are ever to be found in the fountains of quick resolve and swift stroke; and it seems to be a law inflexible and inexorable that he who will not risk cannot win."

Risk we did. We turned up the heat and prepared to sweat it out.

Chapter Twenty-four
Bleeding Bill Allen

Like many Alaskans, "Big Ed" Dankworth was a larger-than-life character: lawman and lawmaker—even a lawbreaker, some said. He'd worked his way up through the ranks to become commander of the Alaska State Troopers, retired from that job and been elected to the state House of Representatives. He later moved up to the twenty-member Alaska State Senate. When he left there to cash in as a lobbyist, people called him "the twenty-first senator" on account of his deal-making skills and continuing, expansive influence.

He was about six-foot-four. Over his long career, I had watched his weight fluctuate between about 220 and 280 pounds. He was fond of hand-tooled cowboy boots and, despite having lived in Alaska for decades, always spoke like the boy he had been in Ballinger, deep in the heart of Texas.

He left the Senate under an ethical cloud in 1982 when he was charged with conflict of interest in pushing an appropriation to buy a former pipeline construction camp he'd purchased. Two years later a court of appeals ruled he was protected against the charges by legislative immunity and he ended up even more powerful outside the Senate than he had been in it. He could pick and choose his lobbying clients and so represented a small cadre of the best-paying.

I'd known and liked Ed since my early days as a cop reporter, sharing both his bulk and his fondness for Texas-style barbecue. He made friends easily and amongst all kinds of people, even smart-aleck reporters. "You'd make a pretty good trooper son," he told me once. "If you lost some weight, that is, and stopped smokin' that pot."

Over the years we continued to meet from time to time at The BBQ Pit or other out-of-the-way restaurants where we were unlikely to run into his Republican friends and clients. I always thought there was some real affection on both sides; in any case, we definitely were useful to one another. He'd given me a boost on some of my earliest investigations; twenty years later, he was now about to let me in on an even bigger secret.

One of his high-paying clients in those days was Bill Allen, whose Veco company had plenty of interests in Juneau that needed looking after. Years later Ed would ditch Veco because Allen insisted Ed choose between representing Veco or another client Allen didn't like. As the high-powered scandals of later years would demonstrate, picking the other guy and dumping Bill Allen was surely one of Big Ed's better decisions.

When Ed and I met for lunch one day in the spring of 1992, he and Allen were still tight and I knew Ed was looking after his client. Soon enough the conversation turned to the newspaper war.

He asked me how I thought the battle was going, and I allowed as how we were winning and likely would triumph within a few years. Two years and tens of millions of dollars after Allen's purchase of the *Times*, Allen had managed to narrow our daily circulation lead by just 2,000 (we were still ahead by 23,000) and we'd actually widened our lead on Sunday, where the big advertising dollars were.

It all depends on how long Allen wants to lose money, I said.

"Well, you know, you boys are bleedin' ol' Bill Allen pretty good," he said.

"He can make that stop any time he wants to," I replied "All he has to do is quit."

Dankworth responded with uncharacteristic seriousness. "He'd never do that. He wouldn't give up his editorial page."

I had read some time before about an innovative arrangement in Shreveport, Louisiana where a newspaper competition ended with one paper agreeing to include an editorial page from the other to preserve diversity of opinion after it shut down. It was the first thing that flashed across my mind as I listened.

"Maybe he wouldn't have to. Things like that can be worked out. It's happened before."

We talked a little more and I filled Ed in on what I knew about Shreveport. He seemed interested, but I had no way of guessing then what a big wheel had just started turning. Before it stopped spinning my life—and many others—would change forever.

I felt it start to happen a couple of months later when Jerry Grilly and I sat in his office to take a call from McClatchy CEO Erwin Potts. It came just after lunch on May 18, 1992.

Erwin called to fill us in on a strange new development. A lawyer representing the *Anchorage Times* had telephoned McClatchy's senior vice president Bill Honeysett a few days earlier to say he was calling on behalf of "people who would really like to buy the *Anchorage Daily News*."

Honeysett knew the score and didn't even need to check with Potts before telling Conrad Shumadine that he'd "never heard a whisper here about interest in selling the *Daily News*."

Almost immediately Shumadine changed gears. "We either want to buy you guys or you buy us. We have to do a deal on this or we'll both continue to bleed." He soon made his real proposal plain: "If you're not interested in selling, how about buying us?"

Allen had one "non-negotiable demand," Shumadine added. "The *Times* would "absolutely have to have" an editorial voice in the *Daily News*.

McClatchy execs soon learned Shumadine was an anti-trust specialist who had represented the winning side when the Little Rock, Arkansas newspaper war was settled. His client in that deal, a friend of Erwin's, described the lawyer as "very honest, very tough, very smart." This strange proposal that had come out of the blue was starting to sound serious.

I had told Erwin about my Dankworth conversation shortly after it occurred, though neither of us thought much about it at the time. Now Erwin floated an idea: how about offering Allen an op-ed page five days a week, his to fill as he saw fit subject only to our right to reject anything we thought libelous. Erwin initially suggested the page be offered "in perpetuity," but I cautioned against that, suggesting that Shreveport's agreement was durational and ours should be, too.

I walked away from the phone call a little shell shocked but nevertheless thinking this might really presage the end of the *Times*. I quickly typed out a memo for the file about the call we'd just concluded, and I kept that up throughout the negotiations. I kept the memos hidden on my Macintosh under the code name "Greyhound" after a quote from Shakespeare's Henry V that sprang to mind: "I see you stand like greyhounds in the slips, straining upon the start. The game's afoot...")

Erwin Potts called back in about two hours—3:15 pm, my second memo of the day says—to describe the conversation he'd just had with Conrad Shumadine. The game was definitely afoot: the *Anchorage Times* wants to sell to us and they want an op-ed page, Erwin said. They want us to make them an offer. And they want to move fast.

Two days later Erwin had talked to his lawyers and the McClatchy board and was ready to return Shumadine's call. He checked in with us and outlined what he planned to say.

My memo about that call says "Erwin plans to tell ... Shumadine that he has discussed the possibility of purchasing the *Times* with his board... The message will be that we are not uncomfortable with the current situation—we are winning, we have demonstrated that we can meet or beat any strategy [Allen] comes up with, surely he has seen that in two years. On the other hand, this is a costly fight and if that could be worked out it would be for the best. Erwin plans to stress that he is not offering 'a come-out position' to start the bargaining, but rather a 'first, last and best offer' that is good for one week. He'll tell them, 'There is no point in coming back in a week with a counter offer.' "

The deal that emerged was simple enough: after the *Times* folded, we would buy the paper's assets — land, building, press— and its circulation and advertiser lists. Bill Allen would agree not to compete in the future, and nobody after him could use the name "*Anchorage Times.*"

And we made a generalized proposal: Allen could also have "an editorial voice in our pages" for three years.

The McClatchy board of directors was ready to keep fighting but agreed that "a quick and advantageous settlement" was better, though it did not like the idea of the *Times* having a voice on our op-ed page and suggested instead that we offer space *in addition* to our existing opinion pages.

Later that day Erwin Potts talked to Shumadine, who said he was authorized to negotiate on Veco's behalf. Veco wanted to keep the *Times'* downtown building. Erwin said fine, McClatchy was not in the real-estate business—but our offer would be smaller. When the deal was finished, both parties agreed to keep the purchase price confidential, and so far as I know the price never has been revealed publicly. I can tell you this much: it wasn't large.

Something close to a final deal was concluded in Erwin's next conversation that day with the Veco lawyer: the *Times* would close on its own, and subsequently we would purchase some of the assets. To this day most people who remember the deal still describe it as *ADN* "buying and closing" the *Times.* That's wrong.

The *Times* itself helped incubate that version, reporting incorrectly in its last edition that "The *Anchorage Times* was sold for an undisclosed price to McClatchy ..." The *Daily News* story got it right.

They approached us. The idea for a sale was theirs and the decision to fold was theirs. We talked when they called, and listened when they made us an offer it would have been imprudent to refuse.

The *Anchorage Times* decision to fold came as nearly a complete surprise in Anchorage—even to the staffs at both newspapers. It was a landmark event in Alaska journalism history, but surprisingly devoid of drama as we lived through the actual events.

Once terms were reached, Bill Allen moved swiftly to cut his losses. On Wednesday morning, June 3, 1992 the *Times* appeared with a giant one-word headline: FAREWELL.

Unsurprisingly, a number of *Times* staffers cried when they heard the news that morning. They might have been surprised to learn that, following a brief cheer when the news was announced; plenty of tears flowed among our staffers, too.

Jerry Grilly and I called an all-hands meeting on the morning of the announcement and when employees had gathered on the loading dock. I made a short statement.

"It would be disingenuous of me to pretend that I am not proud ... of all that we, together, have done. But I also recollect what I have said a hundred times in the last 20 years: that our objective in this battle was not to replace Robert Atwood's voice with ours. Our objective was not to replace Bill Allen's voice with ours.

"Our dream has been focused on our own performance. Our dream is to publish a newspaper that speaks for the whole community, including the people without powerful voices. Our dream is to treat all people equally. Our dream is to produce a newspaper that truly serves this community without fear and without favor."

Newspaper failures are more common now, but they weren't then. The loss of the *Anchorage Times*, for so long the dominant voice of the Anchorage establishment and a relentless promoter of development, sent shock waves around Alaska.

•••

In the end the biggest complication had come not over money or timing or how to characterize the deal. It came over the op-ed proposal, which Shumadine described as "the most important single thing in the whole deal to [Allen]."

It had ended in a compromise: half an op-ed page for Veco, with something less than absolute editorial freedom.

Jerry and I had pushed at the last moment for a tougher deal. My memo asked Erwin:

"Will we have the right to edit for taste? Could Bill Allen's page say "The governor ought to go fuck himself"?

"Could their page appear with an attack against a candidate on the day of the election, a practice we would never allow in our paper?

"Can they use their space like a news page, printing stories or investigations we can't in any way vouch for but which carry, to some inevitable degree, our imprimatur?"

Sacramento acknowledged similar concerns, but Erwin Potts ultimately hung his hat on language inserted into the contract that said if we thought they were violating journalistic standards, we could decline to publish until the issue was reviewed by an ad hoc panel of "three distinguished editors" selected from outside the company.

Allen found that "insulting," his lawyer said.

"Tell him to produce a quality page and he'll never have to worry about that," Erwin countered. Yet quality was never Veco's objective, and it turned out we were the ones who should have worried.

Having lived through Veco's *Voice of the Times,* which stained the *Daily News*, I wish I'd had more doubts or reservations at the time of the deal, or that my cautionary arguments had been more persuasive. Instead I now live with the knowledge that the idea probably originated with me—that the seed got planted in Allen's conniving mind on account of my conversation with Big Ed.

That hurts.

Leaving the *Voice of the Times* in Bill Allen's hands turned out to be far worse than letting a fox loose in your henhouse. It was more like letting an oil slick loose in Prince William Sound.

Some day the full story of Allen's sordid life and reports of how he purchased friends, politicians, and teenage girls will be written as a book of its own; it richly deserves the best of efforts.

The gross outline of his story is known already, much of it written by reporter Rich Mauer and others at the *Anchorage Daily News*. We now know without doubt what kind of criminal and pervert we had accepted as a partner; because I was instrumental in leaving him that platform, that evidence belongs here with my story as well.

In the early 1990s Allen already was demonstrably sleazy, having committed the largest campaign-finance violation in Alaska history. He was thuggish by reputation, in the oilfields and elsewhere. He was crude and profane and often drunk.

All that was nothing compared to what we learned later. Though he would sometimes stay in the home of a U.S. senator who called him a friend, Allen's was fundamentally a story of small-time bribery repeated on an epic scale. He would be captured on many hours of FBI surveillance video in crude and felonious behavior in a Juneau hotel suite. "I own your ass," he would proclaim—truthfully—to one elected representative.

Even that wasn't the worst.

All the while, several young women alleged later, darker and more disgusting sins were taking place hidden from public view, out of sight in warehouses and hotel suites, in automobiles, and his own home, sometimes with teenage girls.

Anchorage police had learned as early as 2004 about a teen-ager who said she had been prostituted by Bill Allen. Federal authorities may have quashed that line of investigation by local law enforcement because it didn't fit with the government corruption case they were mainly pursuing at the time—the one in which Bill Allen would flip and become the key witness for the feds, ratting out nearly everybody else involved, including U.S. Senator Ted Stevens.

Then, in 2008, another witness came forward. The girl spelled out her part of the story for authorities.

Here's what she told an Anchorage police detective:

Allen first picked her up, she said, cruising in a white Land Rover or Range Rover when she had just started working as a prostitute in the fall of 1999. She was fifteen. She remembers it was cold, but that there was no snow on the ground yet.

Allen paid her $200 for sex that time, she told police, and later offered more money for intercourse without a condom. They had sex in a camper stored in an Anchorage warehouse—presumably Allen's—in hotel rooms, and at Allen's house, where he and the girl once crossed paths with a man Allen said was his son. After she moved to Seattle, Allen paid her $2,000 per trip to return to Anchorage for sex in the Hilton and other hotels.

He wanted a "threesome" and badgered her about it until she found another teenage girl to participate. He asked for some other unconventional sex, but she refused, the woman told police.

Allen gave her gifts and spending money and several times wired her more cash after she moved to Seattle. He also bought alcohol and delivered it to the girl's mother in a Muldoon trailer park because she "liked to drink a lot," the girl recalled.

Allen's sexual habits never led to criminal charges. In November 2001 the *Anchorage Daily News* reported, "An effort by state prosecutors to pursue a case against former Veco Corp. chief Bill Allen on allegations of child sexual abuse has ended with no charges…Richard Svobodny, the state's deputy attorney general over criminal matters, said that unless new information materializes—or there's a prosecution on federal charges—the matter is essentially closed."

I know of no more disgusting story in the annals of Alaska politics and journalism.

The Anchorage detective who asked the teenage prostitute if she was afraid to tell her story recorded this poignant, somewhat plaintive reply: "[S]he said she felt a little unsafe because she knew guys with money could do anything they wanted."

Meanwhile, Allen's publishing deal with the *Daily News* was contractually renewed after the five years and then voluntarily extended for another five.

That legacy marked a low point for the *News.*

And, of course, for me.

Chapter Twenty-five
My new narrative

And so, in 1992, the story ended—except it didn't.
When Bill Allen folded the *Anchorage Times* and walked away it had been almost exactly twenty years since I returned to Alaska from college and enlisted in a crusade to create journalism worthy of what Alaska meant to me. In that time I'd climbed from foot soldier to field marshal, from insurgent to incumbent, from underdog to victor—but I had always been in the fight.

Now I was tired and disoriented. Though we'd won what I thought was lasting security for the *Daily News* and its fiercely independent journalism, the absence of the *Times* was oddly haunting. After dominating the landscape for so long, having it suddenly disappear overnight felt like waking up to find a peak from the Chugach Mountains gone missing. A large part of how I'd defined myself simply was no longer there.

I was worn out. I'd been the boss more than half of my career, a responsibility that weighed heavily on my sense of self. I am by nature questioning, avoid dogma, and am not given to easy judgments. I got sick to my stomach when we fired people, suffered in silence and isolation through fights with publishers and sweated through sleepless nights trying to design win-win solutions for feuding colleagues. I always worried about making the One Big Mistake that would bring all our accomplishments tumbling down around us. I liked being editor and it was deeply rewarding, but none of this came easy or painlessly.

In the midst of some firestorm or another, Cathy Janvrin, who handled letters to the editor, stopped by my office with the latest batch of criticisms, which I routinely okayed for publication.

"I don't see how such a nice guy can be so tough," she told me.

"It's all an act," I replied. She smiled at my apparent joke, but in truth I was serious.

I've always believed we live our lives—consciously or not— according to a script spelled out in a personal inner narrative. Everybody has one, and for me it had long been a simple, powerful old standard: "Poor Boy Makes Good."

I'd worked my way up out of Muldoon to prove something, to myself and others. I championed egalitarian values because I lived them; fair is fair, damn it, and everybody ought to have an honest shot and a chance to speak up. I believed in the old saw about "comforting the afflicted and afflicting the comfortable," and I did both every chance I got.

I had started with a powerful need for approval, but that wasn't my driver any more. Outside the meritocracy of our newsroom I didn't respect many people enough to care anymore if they liked me. I did, however, want them to pay attention.

Now the *Times* was gone; more than gone, vanquished. Our little paper up north of nowhere had won the Pulitzer Prize Gold Medal for Public Service twice, a shocking upset of journalistic expectations. The paper was now owned by a company whose values I trusted and respected. I was making more money than I'd ever imagined. Hell, McClatchy even bought me a company car; the first one I selected was a bright red Saab Turbo with butterscotch leather seats. When I took a television newsman for a ride he told me, "It's like riding around in a catcher's mitt."

"Poor Boy Makes Good" was wearing a little thin. Now a new narrative competed for my attention: "What's Next?"

I played for time, taking a year off work to earn a master's degree. Instead of the fellowship route taken by many mid-career journalists, I enrolled as a regular grad student and went back to school on my own nickel, paying tuition and earning a degree from Cambridge University in England.

The McClatchy brass were accommodating about my request for a sabbatical. I gave up my salary but they kept my insurance and benefits going and held my job. I promised to return.

A Fairbanks friend had told me about a Cambridge program focused on "polar studies"—a mélange of history, science, and cultural studies involving the north and south polar regions. It was perhaps the smallest program available at Cambridge (eight people maximum each year) in one of the ancient university's most obscure divisions – the Scott Polar Research Institute. No doubt that sounds narrow and arcane, but I was editing a northern newspaper, after all, and the program was constructed perfectly for a generalist like me—a few weeks each to study climatology, the history of polar explorations, cultures of indigenous peoples, and so forth.

The program also offered a quick route to a prestigious-sounding new degree. At Cambridge and a few other elite British schools, the Master of Arts degree automatically follows with no additional work for everyone who graduates with a bachelor's degree. To differentiate the *earned* master's degree, it comes with a different name: Master of Philosophy. Now that sounded cool: a Master of Philosophy degree from Cambridge University, home of Isaac Newton (gravity, calculus), Watson & Crick (DNA), and the Cavendish lab (splitting of the atom).

I learned a great deal and had some fun in Cambridge despite growing to despise the suffocating English class system and the university's pervasive elitism, but I saw the degree mainly as another notch on my poor-boy-makes-good gunbelt.

What I never imagined was how fast the world of security and stability I'd envisioned for the *Daily News* began to erode while I was out of the country.

The biggest changes started when Publisher Jerry Grilly was promoted to a new job in Sacramento and McClatchy announced that Fuller Cowell would take that job.

When told of the impending change I took it as an encouraging development. Over the years I had often become weary of my high-maintenance publisher and figured the new guy would be easier to deal with. He had Alaska roots and came with the backing of executives I trusted in the corporate office.

By chance he was visiting England while I was still in school there and we met in London just before he moved to Anchorage ahead of my return. It was a pleasant encounter and our conversation reinforced my hopes.

However, disappointment was on the near horizon. I got back to Anchorage and immediately heard complaints about his leadership style, which seemed pretty much the opposite of Grilly's. Newsroom staffers found him stiff and unapproachable. "If I took a photo with infra-red film, do you think he would show up?" one asked me.

Yet newsroom bitching about publishers was hardly a new phenomenon, and I settled in to start building the kind of trust essential for any great publisher-editor relationship.

We never got there.

We had some skirmishes right away. I had enjoyed autonomy during the Grilly years that infringed on Fuller's expectations. To put it bluntly, he thought he was the boss in all respects. I didn't.

Stories about editors and publishers clashing over independence are a well-worn cliché in the news business. I see no value in revisiting all of ours here, though I was troubled enough to keep detailed memos to the file recording them at the time.

In one respect, our differences were especially stark and lasting. Fuller expected as publisher to be the final authority on the paper's editorial positions; had he been allowed to do so, he would have reversed decades of policy regarding everything from abortion rights to sovereignty for Alaska Natives.

McClatchy's longtime practice (like that of most quality news companies) held that the editorial voice of the paper was greater than that any one individual, generally subject to the kind of historical continuity one finds in jurisprudence. Yes, laws (and editorial positions) can change, but not capriciously. The default is in favor of precedent.

I had enough stature in Sacramento to resist Fuller's intentions for the editorial page, though he was consistent and persistent in his efforts to change things. We crossed swords not only over hot-button questions such as abortion but also on topics I could hardly believe he'd mention, including his opposition to the United Nations or what I saw as his extreme defense of state's rights. He often recommended that I read *Atlas Shrugged*, Ayn Rand's magnum opus of objectivism and "rational selfishness" that has become a foundation document for the politics of laissez-faire capitalism. He kept a bust of Robert E. Lee in his office; after I asked about it, he added another of Abraham Lincoln.

He also distrusted the newsroom's aggressive style of journalism. He once expressed outrage over the notion that the newspaper should "comfort the afflicted and afflict the comfortable." It was appalling, he told me, to talk about targeting people just because they were successful and comfortable.

I didn't tell him I'd been using that quote in public speeches for years—but neither did I take it out.

All this made returning to my job as editor far less satisfying than I'd expected. Two years after my return from Cambridge all I could foresee was a future of fighting Fuller to a standstill on issue after issue, working in an environment now resistant to the kind of aggressive journalism and innovation we were known for. I was in my early forties and couldn't see myself spending another twenty years doing that.

Moreover, I had some ambition left that was feeding a new "what's next?" narrative in my life. I knew I had a reasonable chance of becoming McClatchy's VP for news—the chief editorial officer—when incumbent Gregory Favre retired. I wanted to be in a position to try for that.

Far earlier than most newspaper people in those days I recognized that the Internet would transform journalism. On a personal website I built in 1995, I had declared, "I don't know where the web, the net, or the cosmos is headed, but I'm certain they're on track to the future. I've always been a storyteller, and I'm convinced the stories of the new millennium will be told digitally."

So it was that when CEO Erwin Potts offered me the chance to spend a year helping craft the company's new media strategy and then work in Sacramento as heir-apparent for the top news job, I said yes.

As a lifelong Alaska patriot I never expected to live anywhere else, yet leaving the state was surprisingly easy. Leaving the *Daily News*, by contrast, was a nightmare.

Against all logic and my every expectation, the company did not promote Pat Dougherty to be editor when I left. In addition to having been lead editor on our latest Pulitzer-winning series and a recent Nieman Fellow at Harvard, he had proved his capacity for the job splendidly by running things for nine months while I was at Cambridge. What better resume, complete with a nine-month test drive? Naively, I took his promotion as a given.

Instead, the corporate office selected Kent Pollock, a Favre protégé from the *Sacramento Bee*, a stinging disappointment to me and crushing blow to Patrick. I was out of town at a new media conference when the deal went down and tried to call Pat. We didn't connect and I wrote one of the saddest emails of my career:

"I am desperately sorry they didn't pick you, and desperately sorry for the pain you feel and for my role in it. It hurts me to think that I am profiting—improving my lot—while yours is getting worse ... I don't know what the future will bring; neither do you. I have faith that it will not be as black as you think or last as long as you now fear. You have always been a fighter; these are still the middle rounds, Patrick. If you keep your head and your cool, there are still a lot of alternative endings to explore."

Pat responded with unbelievable grit and determination. Fortunately for McClatchy and the newsroom, he was still there, ready to become editor, when Pollock flamed out a couple of years later. Since then, he's led the paper with distinction through the most turbulent period in its history.

Fuller's departure from the publisher's job about three years after I left was marked by tragedy and courage. Fuller was diagnosed with leukemia and successfully fought back with dogged determination. I admire him for that and other accomplishments, but for me his legacy at the *Daily News* is that he worked hard during his tenure to reverse many of the paper's journalistic accomplishments and shift its editorial philosophy radically to the right.

Pollock's hiring, Fuller's tenure, and the paper's continuing willingness to publish Bill Allen's *Voice of the Times* all served to remind me unambiguously that the *Anchorage Daily News* was not my newspaper.

I had been entrusted with its guidance for many years, the greatest opportunity of my life, but in the end had fallen prey to a kind of self-deception well known in business and politics. H.G. Wells had described this perfectly long ago: "It is the universal weakness of mankind that what we are given to administer, we presently imagine we own."

Thus in October 1995 I arrived in Sacramento with the longest title and perhaps the best assignment in the company: "assistant to the president for new media strategies," working for one of the few newspaper executives I ever admired unambiguously, CEO-to-be Gary Pruitt. I had free rein and a year's time to explore an important subject that fascinated me. I traveled across the country interviewing experts and observing nascent online efforts, ending the year with a report to the board of directors and, later, to all McClatchy editors and publishers. Looking at it today, I'm proud to have gotten so much of it right in that early era.

As Erwin had foreseen when we talked about my future, I then moved on the *Sacramento Bee*'s editorial pages and later served as vice president for news from 2001-2008. Another narrative was ready to begin for me and with it came other stories.

Epilogue

L ooking back at what's come to be known as the Great Alaska Newspaper War, I find that I remember three artifacts that represent distinctly different periods.

The first is a rock, picked up from an alley behind the *Anchorage Times* late one August night in 1974 and drunkenly hurled toward the glass of a second-story window there. It exists only in my memory now.

The second is tangible and still sits on my desk: a strangely shaped piece of burnished aluminum about the size of an ashtray that once represented Nunivak Island, part of a giant outline of Alaska decorating the front of that *Times* building. It was pried off somehow in the middle of one night in the mid-1980s by a number of people who then worked for me. They left it on my desk with a message, "Just to remind you what kind of people we are."

The third is a large Alaska flag that once flew atop the *Times* and now hangs where I can see it from the window as I write this at Redwing Ranch in California's Sierra foothills. Unlike the stolen Nunivak Island, I came by this trophy honestly, claiming it from the assets the *Times* sold after they folded and admitted defeat in 1992.

We had won. I wanted their flag and I got it. Juvenile, you think? If only Robert B. Atwood had worn a uniform; I would have ripped off his epaulettes and broken his sword across my knee.

•••

I didn't understand this at the time but I came to realize that I had turned my back on Alaska mainly because it broke my heart.

Alaska's slow but steady corruption by the oil industry had been confirmed beyond all doubt when citizens rolled over in the aftermath of *Exxon Valdez* to embrace the industry and its corrupt champions all over again.

The crude and criminal Bill Allen was celebrated as Alaskan of the Year, surrounded by politicians he'd bought and paid for, entertaining visiting delegations of U.S. senators and basking in the sycophancy of the state's greedy establishment. His son was investing earnings from Veco's corrupt business in a horse-racing enterprise that would bring him a Kentucky Derby winner.

Fuller Cowell was whittling away steadily at the independence and initiative of the *ADN*, reducing its outsized aspirations to something closer to his own size and constrained expectations.

And as hard as we worked so many years, in the end we hadn't managed to change any of that nearly enough.

I had taken up a crusader's banner two decades before to fight for things I believed in: my parents' naive idealism; the romance and history that made Alaska special; proof that poor boys could make good; and most of all, an enduring belief that telling the truth would change things—that people would make good choices if only they understood.

To one degree or another, I left with all those illusions dimmed or tarnished. I hadn't given up—after all, I was on my way to a new adventure on a new, electronic frontier—but my faith that the human spirit turned instinctively toward the light was shaken. It sure hadn't worked that way in Alaska.

After years of distance and reflection, I now see the lessons I learned there are part of a much bigger story. Yes, the Alaska I treasured has been corrupted, its legendary pioneers replaced too often with scoundrels and second-raters. For all its success, our newspaper failed to prevent that. But there was much more at play.

Because Alaska is the last frontier for a nation defined by frontier expansion, the changes I lived through there both reflected and presaged epic changes in the United States as a whole. The shorthand for that dynamic can be reduced to "Sarah Palin," who was not responsible for Alaska's deterioration but is supremely representative of it.

That story of disappearing frontier and eroding culture itself deserves to be illuminated, a task I hope to undertake now that this deeply personal view of the Alaska Newspaper War has been presented.

Author's note

The "A People in Peril" series and the Pulitzer Prize it won
reflected an outstanding tradition of public service journalism by the *Anchorage Daily News*, particularly the focus
on Alaska Native people the newspaper had sustained for almost
twenty-five years.

Four special projects—each of them still an illuminating
document—are the anchors of that coverage: "The Village People,"
published in December 1965; "The Emerging Village People" in
December 1967; "The Village People Revisited" in 1981; and, in
1988, "A People In Peril."

None of these were ordinary newspaper journalism. After the
first was published in December 1965, staffers felt compelled to
break with tradition and tell readers not only what they'd learned,
but what they thought about it.

> It had not been our intention to conclude this series with
> recommendations. Our purpose has been to inform read-
> ers about the Alaska Native·...
>
> But after months of study, travel and conversation, we
> have formed some opinions and ideas. These we must
> publish also.

In [Native] areas poverty is a way of life—perhaps as deeply embedded as in any place under the American flag. Welfare checks take the place of jobs. Though there are schools, educational achievement remains low. Alcohol and tuberculosis take a tremendous toll. Most homes are substandard. There is a high expectation of failure among the population.

... What exists today is self evident proof that the present system is not sufficient. Decades of good intentions have not produced notable results.

... And it is not enough to say that the people must help themselves. The Native people of Alaska have been among the most self-reliant on earth—their climate and way of life demanded it. What they lack now are the tools for becoming self-reliant in the new culture.

That series attracted national attention. A month after publication, the Alaska Legislature asked Congress for help, and by February 1966 a commission impaneled by President Lyndon Johnson reported back on needs across the state and said the Yukon-Kuskokwim Delta region in particular "presents such a problem of human distress and misery that it must be considered separately and urgently." Much of rural Alaska, the commission found, was "a land without a foothold in the 20th century."

In December 1967, shortly after Larry and Kay Fanning bought the *Daily News*, the paper once more mounted an out-sized effort, sending its small staff out to crisscross the state again to survey conditions amongst Native people. They called that report "The Emerging Village People," and declared in the introduction, "The story told in 'The Village People' did not end with the last installment. It is a continuing struggle by the Native people of Alaska to find a way to survive their collision with western culture,"

I was managing editor when the paper undertook its third in-depth examination in December 1981, producing another comprehensive series that drew its name from the legacy of previous efforts: "The Village People Revisited."

More than twenty staffers worked on that project, which was launched by an overview story I wrote outlining our findings:

> It is quiet in the villages of Bush Alaska, but not silent.
>
> There is a constant rumble from the generator in Kiana and the noise of a fuel truck making deliveries in Anaktuvuk Pass. There is a distant whine of snow machines along the trail from Chevak to Hooper Bay. In Shungnak the televised bark of gunfire and wail of sirens leaks out beneath a doorway into the afternoon darkness, an echo of urban entertainment bounced off a satellite in orbit 22,300 miles above the earth.
>
> These are the sounds of change winds blowing ... Alaska's Eve has tasted technology's apple, and there is no turning back.

The title "A People in Peril" was likewise a conscious tribute to the reporting of the past. The Pulitzer we won for this work reflected the increasing sophistication and skill we could bring to bear on a difficult, complex, and controversial subject.

It also reflected the contributions of C.K. McClatchy, who not only rescued the *Daily News* but also sustained and nourished the spirit of public service journalism that had long animated the paper.

On April 17, 1989, less than three weeks after the Pulitzer announcement, he died suddenly and unexpectedly.

I wrote a column of appreciation and regret a few days later.

> As late as 36 hours before he died of a heart attack while jogging, I had sat in quiet celebration at his table at the American Society of Newspaper Editors and plotted future adventures. He had been the happy and deserving center of much attention at that conference, where his lifelong

commitment to quality newspapers, local autonomy and decent behavior had come very much into vogue...

A lot of people have money in this world; fewer are people of high ideals. C.K. McClatchy was one of too few who had both and were willing to put both into play in the contest for a better world.

Acknowledgments

This work owes its existence to many generous friends and advisers. Chief amongst them is my wife and foremost editor, Barbara Hodgin; she shares in the creation of this book no less than in the life I have lived since meeting her.

Sharon Palmisano, once the dedicated librarian at the *Anchorage Daily News*, took time from a precious Alaska summer to help me research the book both in dusty drawers and on flickering computer screens. Its accurate grounding is a tribute to her skill; its mistakes of course are my own.

Several early and late readers helped me steer this story to the conclusion it finds here. Joe Acton, John Greely, John Larson, and Stewart McBride brought distinct and essential perspectives to their thoughtful appraisals. Former colleagues Kim Rich, Amy Quinn, and Kim Severson were quick to offer support and advice, all of it valuable, some of it irreplaceable. James McGinniss' early support and enthusiasm gave me confidence.

As it did so often during the course of my career, John McKay's advice and support buoyed my confidence and corrected my course.

Many *ADN* alumni showed alacrity and generosity in offering advice, support and often materials to help. Jeanne Abbott provided access to a personal photo collection of invaluable utility, and Elaine Warren likewise was generous in sharing both images and insights. Bill Kossen crossed the ancient divide between the *Anchorage Times* and *Daily News* to share photos illuminating the story from a perspective wholly different than my own.

I developed an email network of friends and colleagues throughout the late stages of my work to test ideas and solicit advice, something that would have been impossible to do in a timely way before we were all connected through the internet. Their alacrity warmed my heart and improved my writing. I can't imagine ever doing something like this again without similar consultation. Thank you, book-mates; you know who you are.

Finally, I am grateful to Kent Sturgis at Epicenter Press, who had the faith to undertake this project with me and the skill to help shape it along the way.

Index

Page numbers for photos are in **bold**.

-A-

"A People In Peril," 105, 131, 133, 171, 227, 229

Abbott, Jeanne, 16, **89**, 231

Abbott, Stan, 18, 37, 54, 61, **87**, **88**, **89**, 96-97, 105-107

Alaska Advocate, 7, 62-84, 91-95, 109,129, 138, 146, 155

Alaska Future Society, 156

Alaska Legislature, 54, 56, 61, 62, 75, 93, 145, 176, 183, 228

Alaska Library Association, 160

Alaska Natives, 32, 105, 138, 174-178, 218, 227

Alaska Supreme Court, 76, 77, 145, 183

Alexander, Bill, 197

Allen, Bill, 189-201, 205-207, 209-213, 215, 224

Andrews, Clint, 31

Arco, 81, 192

Atwood, Elaine, 23

Atwood, Robert B., 24-35, 50, 70, 90, 91, 108-109, **181**, 189-190, 199, 224

-B-

Babb, James D., 54, **89**

Bailey, Terry, 71

Baum, Danny, 186

Bergmann Hotel, 57

Berry, Mary Clay, 32

Bolles, Don, 46

Bonanno organized crime family, 40, 47

Bowditch, Molly, 15

Boyko, Edgar Paul, 76-77

Breslin, Jimmy, 55, 122, 166

British Petroleum, 147, 193

Brown, Kay, 72

Brown, Tom, 16

Bryson, George, 113

Buonmassa, Peter Rosario, 53
Burnham, David, 38
Byron, Don, **186**

-C-
Cambridge University, 217,
   219-220
Campbell, Mike, 114, 173, **185**
Carey, Michael, 133, 150
Carlson, Gordon "Satch", 73
Carr, Jesse L., 50-52
Christian Science Monitor, 99, 104,
   106, 107
Coblentz, Bill, 95, 106
CompuServe, 156
Conklin, Ellis E., 186
Cowell, Fuller, 218-219, 221, 224
Cowper, Steve, 69
Craigslist, 162-163
Cuddy, Dan, 63

-D-
Dankworth, Ed, 205, 207-208
Dickey, Fred, 190
Doogan, Mike, 133, 148-149, 172,
   194
Dougherty, Katie, 130
Dougherty, W.P. Pat, 72, 113, 121-
   123, 129-130, 133, 135-136, 154,
   173-174, 179, **185**, 220
Doyle, Diana, **92**
Dunlap-Shohl, Peter, 142, 182
Dylan, Bob, 50, 75

-E-
"Empire: the Alaska Teamsters
   Story," 51, 54
Enstar, 193
environment, environmentalists,
   30, 31, 75-79, 108-109, 187, 189,
   194
Erickson, Jim, 66, **92**
Exxon, 189, 193, 196, 197
Exxon Valdez oil spill, 82, 133, 187,
   189-193, 224

-F-
Fanning, Kay, 35-37, 52-54, **86**, **89**,
   90, 97-99, 103-105, 109, 114,
   179, **180**, 228, 239
Favre, Gregory, 119, 220
Field, Ted, 61
Figone, Fred Dominic, 53
Fineberg, Richard, 69
Fishburn, Dudley, 137
Frank, Allan Dodds, 16, 20-21

-G-
Gibboney, Tom, 16, 54
Goodrich, Paul, 65, 147
Greely, John, 58, 62, 64, 66, 68, 77,
   83, **92**, 231
Greene, Bob, 38
Grilly, Gerald E., 98-99, 101, 155,
   174, **181**, 201, 207, 210, 218
Groh, Clifford John, 73, 77, 84, **93**
Gruenstein, Peter, 109

-H-
Halberstam, David, 124-125
Hamel, Charles, 194
Hamiltom, Mark, 83, **92**
Hammond, Jay S., 69, 76-77
Hanrahan, John, 109
Haycox, Steven, 78
Hazelwood, Joe, 187
Heikes, Drex, **186**, 190
Hemingway, Ernest, 84, 122
Herring, Eileen, **92**
Hickel, Ermalee, 25
Hickel, Walter J., 65, 76-77
Hildigard, Jolene, **92**
Hodgin, Barbara, 3, 54, 63, **89**, **94**,
    172, 231, 237
Honeysett, Bill, 207
House, Bernard, 53
Huhndorf, Roy, 32
Hulen, David, 139
Humphrey, Jeanette, 72, **92**

-I-
Iditarod Trail Sled Dog Race, 132,
    182
Internet, 64, 84, 163, 220, 232

-J-
Jacobs, Locke, 30
Janvrin, Cathy, 216
Johns Hopkins University, 33
Joint Operating Agreement (JOA),
    34, 62, 90, 96, 117
Jones, John Paul, 204

-K-
Kenyon, Peter, **183**
Kizzia, Tom, 130, 138
Kurtz, Howard, 194

-L-
Land claims (Native), 30, 32
Lazarus, Bill, 77, **92**
Legislature, see Alaska Legislature
Lew, Karen, **92**
Linda's Massage Parlor, 20
Lindback, John, 144
Local 959, see Teamsters Local 959
Los Angeles Times, 50, 97, 141, 186

-M-
Makinson, Larry, 155, **182**
Martin, Jack, 53
Mauer, Richard, 131, 173-174, **182**,
    185, 195-196, 212
McClatchy Company, 96, 115, 129,
    159, 163, 164, 184, 200-201,
McClatchy Newspapers, 84, 106,
    116, 180
McClatchy, C.K., **90**, 95, 106-109,
    116-119, 178, 229-230
McCoy, Kathleen, 132-133, 173
McCulloch, Frank, 110, 119, 202
McGinniss, James, 231
McGinniss, Joe, 63
McKay, John, 73, 145, **183**, 196-
    197, 231
McKinney, Debra, 133
Modig, Doug, 175

Murphy, Richard, 133, 173
Murray, Sherry, **92**

-N-
Natives, see Alaska Natives
Newmark, Craig, 163
Newsweek magazine, 177
Nielson, Gary, 158
Northcountry Journal, 130,
    138-139

-O-
O'Hara, Doug, 133
Oil industry, 70, 79-81, 189, 191-
    192, 194, 200-201, 224
Organized crime, 10, 20, 23, 40, 46

-P-
Painter, Rodger, 62, 69, 84, **93**
Palmisano, Sharon, 231
Pasley, Jerome Max, 40-42, 46-47
Penn, Michael, **183**
"People In Peril," see "A People In
    Peril"
Pipeline, see Trans-Alaska Pipeline
Piper, E.W., **186**
Pollock, Kent, 220-221
Porterfield, Bob, 49, 54, **89**, 104
Potts, Erwin, 107, 119, 207-211,
    220
Predeger, David, **186**
Print magazine, 127
Pruitt, Gary, 221

Pulitzer Prize, 49-56, 61, 63, **89**,
    121, 131, 133, 171, 178-179,
    185, **186**, 188, 200, 216, 220,
    229, 239

-R-
Rasmussen, Eddie, 23
Roberts, Gene, 122, 154
Roberts, Ken, 68, 72, 92, 93
Rosen, Jay, 153
Royko, Mike, 103, 145

-S-
Sacramento Bee, 220, 222
Scandling, Bruce, 83
Sheffield, William, 143-145, 183
Shinohara, Rosemary, 114
Shumadine, Conrad, 207-210
Society of News Design, 127
Spinelli, Salvatore, 40-47
Star, Stephen, 117-118, 200
Statehood, 29, 30, 79, 108, 237
Stevens, Ted, 212
Stockwell, Brad, 92
Strategic planning, *Anchorage
    Daily News*, 98, 116-117, 119,
    149, 159-160, 181, 199, 202
Sun Tzu, 203-204
Sutherlin, Mark, 92

-T-
Tallman, James, 31
Tarrant Bert, 194

Teamsters Union Local 959, 37-38,
    49-54, 104, 170
Tetpon, John, 138, 173
Time magazine, 155, 182
Tobin, William J., 33
Toomey, Sheila, 131, 173, 176, 183,
    185
Trans-Alaska Pipeline, 27, 30, 38,
    40, 47, 69, 81,146-147, 190, 194,
    205
Tribal Fire, *Anchorage Daily News,*
    135-151, 182

-U-
Unocal, 193
Upicksoun, Martha,173

-V-
Veco, 189-200, 206, 209, 211, 213,
    224
"Village People" series, 105,
    227-229
Voice of the Times, 207, 209-211,
    221
Vu-Text, 161

-W-
Warren, Elaine, 16, 20, 39, 87, 231
Weaver, Mark, 62, 67, 72, 92
Williams, Andy, 62, 63, 70
Wolfe, Tom, 58, 68, 122
World Wide Web, WWW, 158, 220

-Z-
Zieger, Gary, 17-18, 27-28

Carl Costas, carlcostas.com

About the author

Howard Weaver was born in Anchorage in 1950 and lived there with brief interruptions for forty-five years. In that time he lived, worked and played across the state—working as a cannery hand and set-netter in Bristol Bay, river-rafting in the Arctic and building a cabin on Kachemak Bay. Mostly, though, he was a newspaper journalist in Anchorage who started covering high school sports events and ended up as editor of the state's largest paper.

Weaver helped lead the *Anchorage Daily News* to two Pulitzer Prizes, hosted a public television program for ten years and was named one of the forty most influential Alaskans in the first forty years of statehood.

He is married to Barbara Hodgin and now lives mostly in Northern California.

Learn more and find contact information at www.howard-weaver.com.

•••

For more photos, links to documents, a searchable database, and a discussion of the themes in this book, visit www.writeharddiefree.com. Readers are invited to add their perspectives, observations, and opinions.

READING RECOMMENDATIONS
for those who enjoy memoirs from Alaska

Bering Sea Blues
> A Crabber's Tale of Fear in the Far North
> Joe Upton, paperback, $14.95

Cold River Spirits
> Whispers from a Family's Forgotten Past
> Jan Harper-Haines, paperback, $14.95

Kay Fanning's Alaska Story
> Memoir of a Pulitzer-Prize Winning Newspaper Publisher
> Kay Fanning, paperback, $17.95

Moments Rightly Placed
> An Aleutian Memoir
> Ray Hudson, paperback, $14.95

On the Edge of Nowhere
> James Huntington & Lawrence Elliott, paperback, $14.95

Raising Ourselves
> A Gwitch'in Coming of Age Story from the Yukon River
> Velma Wallis, paperback, $15.95

Sisters
> Coming of Age & Living Dangerously
> Samme & Aileen Gallaher, paperback, $14.95

Surviving the Island of Grace
> A Life on the Wild Edge of America
> Leslie Leyland Fields, paperback, $17.95

These titles can be found or special-ordered from your local bookstore, or they may be ordered 24 hours a day at 800-950-6663. More Epicenter titles, including many personal stories, may be found at www.EpicenterPress.com.
> Alaska Book Adventures™
> Epicenter Press, Inc.
> www.EpicenterPress.com